S. GRUNDTVIG

Translated and Edited by Ernest D. Nielsen

WHAT CONSTITUTES AUTHENTIC CHRISTIANITY?

N. F. S. GRUNDTVIG

What Constitutes Authentic Christianity?

**Translated by
Ernest D. Nielsen**

FORTRESS PRESS   PHILADELPHIA

Published by Fortress Press in cooperation with the Danish Interest Conference of the Lutheran Church in America and the Jensen Foundation.

Translated from the Danish *Udvalgte Skrifter,* by N. F. S. Grundtvig, ed. Holger Begtrup (Copenhagen: Nordisk Forlag, 1906).

Library of Congress Cataloging in Publication Data

Grundtvig, N. F. S. (Nicolai Frederick Severin), 1783–1872.
  What constitutes authentic Christianity?

  Translation of: Udvaltge skrifter.
  1. Apologetics—19th century. I. Title.
BT1101.G89613 1985   239   84–48728
ISBN 0–8006–1844–0

1411I84 Printed in the United States of America 1–1844

Contents

This translation is dedicated
to the memory of my late wife
A. FRANCES NIELSEN
(1901–1982)

Foreword

In the English-speaking world we have heard and read a great deal about N. F. S. Grundtvig. However since he wrote only in Danish we have not had much of his writing wherein he could speak for himself. Now through a fortunate combination of circumstances we have Grundtvig in English. Dr. Ernest Nielsen, a Grundtvig scholar for many years, is Danish born and had his early education in Denmark. He is unusually well qualified to translate one of Grundtvig's most important writings.

The Danish Interest Conference has encouraged Dr. Nielsen to undertake this considerable task, and the Jensen Foundation has underwritten certain expenses.

In addition, the publisher has shown great interest and given good counsel. For this we thank Fortress Press. There has been a growing interest in recent years in Grundtvig's thought. Grundtvig held an ecumenical perspective to which the American churches can relate. Given all of these happy circumstances, it is indeed a pleasure to see this translation completed and readied for thoughtful reading.

Ronald Jespersen, President
Danish Interest Conference
Lutheran Church in America

Translator's Preface

N. F. S. Grundtvig, who was born in the parsonage at Udby on the island of Seeland, Denmark, on 8 September 1783, ranks among the most outstanding thinkers and leaders in the Lutheran Church. His great contribution to Danish church and folk life, to education, and to theology and history extended far beyond the boundaries of his own country. Hence, it is not accidental that many celebrations of the two-hundredth anniversary of his birth recently took place. Grundtvig was an ardent writer in the fields of history, education, and religion who could be both very creative and polemical; he was a great hymn writer whose hymns for the season of Pentecost are looked upon as the most beautiful and lyrical hymns in Danish. Finally, he was a great preacher who Sunday after Sunday proclaimed "the living Word" to a most faithful congregation. He preached his last sermon only six days before his death on 2 September 1872. Blessed with a long life, he was enabled to see some of the fruits of his love and zeal for the furtherance of humanity and Christianity among his people. He saw a genuine awakening in the life of the church that he loved; and he saw his thoughts and ideas about education for life applied in the establishment of residential schools for young adults, known as the Danish Folk High Schools.

We are witnessing today a growing interest in what Grundtvig's thoughts and ideas possibly may offer to our own thinking and planning in the years ahead. The time is ripe for advancement in making his writings available in English. He was a prolific writer. Briefly, his writings promulgate his thoughts, give the readers a sense of the liveliness of his language, and challenge them to make their own analysis and evaluation of his thoughts. Hence, the translator has made every effort to produce an unabridged translation, faithful to the original Danish text. The work is a twin treatise in defense of Christianity. According to Holger Begtrup, the editor of the first edition, both this treatise and its sequel, entitled *The Truth of Christianity*, give indications of having been written prior to Grundtvig's so-called discovery in 1825 of what he termed "the living Word of Faith."

The translation follows the first edition of 1826 as found in N. F. S. Grundtvig's *Udvalgte Skrifter* (ed. Holger Begtrup [Copenhagen: Nordisk Forlag, 1906], vol. 4). The translator has given a heading for each of the four divisions of the treatise. The divisions mark the successive order in which the treatise originally appeared in the monthly journal of theology, *Theologisk Maanedsskrift*, vol. 4, January, February, March 1826, and vol. 5, June 1826.

The journal was published and edited by N. F. S. Grundtvig and Dr. A. D. Rudelbach. However, Grundtvig relinquished his editorial post when the court placed him under censure on 30 October of that same year. The court case resulting in this censure grew out of Grundtvig's severe attack on Professor H. N. Clausen's latest publication, a comprehensive study entitled *Catholicism and Protestantism's Ecclesiastical Structure, Teaching, and Ritual.* In *The Church's Reply,* also published in 1825, Grundtvig contended that Clausen's views undermined the very church Clausen was expected to serve and strengthen. The court, however, decided against Grundtvig on the grounds that he had used "improper and offensive" language. The following year, the church's one-thousandth anniversary, Bishop J. P. Mynster issued a pastoral letter in which he prohibited the use of any of the hymns that Grundtvig had written or revised especially for this great celebration. The effect of this restriction in the performance of his ministry caused Grundtvig to submit his resignation. At truly great cost to himself and his family, he stepped aside for a period and turned, not unexpectedly, to writing. A royal grant enabled him to visit England, study Anglo-Saxon manuscripts at the universities there, and become acquainted with the growing democratization of England.

In discussions about Grundtvig, the question frequently raised is whether Grundtvig knew Søren Kierkegaard. They knew each other, but they had very little in common. Kierkegaard had a strong resentment toward Grundtvig which always seemed to surface whenever he attended the Vartov Church in Copenhagen to hear Grundtvig preach. He derided Grundtvig because of his many threats over the years to leave the State Church. He wrote:

> Out of sheer goodheartedness, Grundtvig stays where he is; his followers (the Grundtvigians) admire him, the clergy and the whole country praise and thank him because he has no serious intention of upsetting the existing stable condition, but motivated by love for the sick he continues in his pastoral office, enjoys a good income and, in addition, even receives thanks. In short, it seems to me that Grundtvig's stand is absurd. (Quoted by P. G. Lindhardt in *Konfrontation* [Copenhagen: Akademisk Forlag, 1974], 9)

Kierkegaard, it should be remembered, died on 11 November 1855, but Grundtvig was privileged to be able to lead a productive life up to the time of his death on 2 September 1872. The influence of Grundtvig's long ministry at Vartov Church (1839–1872) spread throughout the country. He was an ardent advocate of freedom within the State Church for both the laity and the pastors.

Today his significant contributions as a historian, educational philosopher, poet of songs and hymns, pastor, and theologian are the subject of study by an increasing number of scholars. Grundtvig contributed to and saw the renewal of the life of the Danish country and people on an unprecedented scale.

He knew and frankly reminded his friends that he was not infallible. He knew the effectiveness of the interaction between persons of different interests that results from "evangelical freedom," setting the community of all believers, both lay people and clergy, free to exercise their servanthood rather than aspire to rule over others. Grundtvig was a Christian apologist whose defense of the faith actually inaugurated a new chapter in our understanding of the human and the Christian and their interrelationship. The freedom that he championed for humankind was rooted in his firm belief in the reality of the spirit. If anyone were to ask him what mattered most, he would answer: Life! Thus the phrase "for life's sake" expressed Grundtvig's commitment to the total renewal of his people on many fronts.

1

The Faith of the Fathers

It is, as we all know, an irrefutable fact that what both our forefathers and Martin Luther called the true Christianity—and whereof we find a concise summary in Luther's *Small Catechism*—present-day scholars commonly call false and describe as a blind and corrupt superstition which has no foundation in the New Testament, but has been deduced therefrom only by misunderstanding and faulty interpretation. On the contrary, the scholars contend that the true Christianity, which veritably is found in the New Testament, is in reality identical to what may be obtained through one's own reason. Hence, it is called Christianity only because Jesus Christ once again brought to life those universal, but virtually forgotten or at least distorted truths about God, providence, and immortality, as well as those concerning man's moral duties; and he expressed these truths in a language appropriate to our human power of perception and designated them as a divine revelation which gained entrance for these truths among primitive and impressionable people, who lacked the necessary knowledge to grasp the truth for themselves, with the result that they, like children in intellectual development, had to accept the revelation in blind faith.

It cannot be denied that such is the general situation today in any discussion of Christianity; for one person speaks with contempt, another with gentleness about the faith of our forefathers; one denies the miracles, resurrection, and divinity of Jesus, the other allows these to be judged on their own merit; and, finally, one is of the opinion that there is absolutely not anything new in Christianity, another concedes that there is something new about providence and love for our enemies. As a matter of fact, these diverse views make very little difference, for the great controversy between us and our Christian fore- fathers is undeniably centering upon *the* faith; faith in Jesus Christ as "the power of God for salvation" (Rom. 1:16), and the only condition whereby sinners can find grace from God and obtain salvation. This faith, which our forefathers viewed as their all in all, is commonly rejected today; it is regarded, in part, as a blind and irrational belief and, partly, as a dangerously inhuman and pernicious superstition. Hence, it is absolutely certain that if our forefathers' Christianity were true, then our generation's is false or vice versa, for the acceptance and altera- tion, the extolling and condemnation, and the defense and con- futation of our forefathers' faith in Christ cannot possibly be identical since the one definitely excludes the other.

Inasmuch as it now has become clear to us that there is a great gulf between that which Luther and our forefathers conjointly named Christianity and what scholars today generally designate by the same name, it behooves every person for whom the wisdom that leads to salvation is important to be truly solic- itous about knowing who is right and which Christianity is true! Ostensibly, for many people this question has been stifled from its very inception by the idea that it matters little or nothing which Christianity, the old or the new, is the true and authentic Christianity, provided we definitely know which is the best, the most reasonable, and the most tenable. With great diligence, scholars have sought to make this idea publicly known and acceptable, in the hope that they might suppress the question which disconcerts them, namely, the genuineness of *their* Christianity. On the contrary, this question obviously ought not to be suppressed but answered as clearly as possible to all concerned, for no person who loves the truth can cherish the desire to be called a Christian, if Christianity in its fundamental base is a lie; moreover, there are, indeed, many people in the Christian world who have a partly inherited, strong supposition that the genuine Christianity is true, and that the false consequently is a lie. Besides, we now know — what hardly can be a complete secret to anyone among us — that this supposition about the truth of authentic Christianity is as solidly founded as any assumption possibly can be, for it rests, in fact, on a trustworthy testimony which has been promulgated throughout many centuries; it is a testimony to Christianity's incomparably beneficial and divine influence on humanity. Knowing this and also hearing the advocates of the so-called new Christianity appealing to this great, experience-grounded testimony concerning the merit of Christianity, it becomes obvious that we face a very important question: Which form of Christianity, the new or the old, constitutes authentic Christianity? Manifestly, every scholar who either attempts to suppress or complicate this question ought, at least, to have some misgivings about the genuineness of *his* Christianity.

As a matter of fact, is it not exceedingly difficult even for erudite scholars, and next to impossible for lay persons, to know for certain which form of Christianity is authentic?

Today there is little room for doubting that this represents the inexorable opinion of our theologians. In sharp contrast, the theologians among our forefathers, in their agreement with Luther, contended the very opposite and emphatically claimed that it was the easiest thing in the world for any sincerely motivated person to attain certainty concerning the identity of genuine Christianity. This much, at least, is as clear as the sun at noon, namely, if it really were impossible for ninety-nine out of a hundred persons in any Christian community to know the genuine Christianity from the false, it follows that Christianity could not possibly have been a divine revelation of the way to eternal salvation, for God is no respecter of persons; the soul of a farmer must inevitably be equally as precious, in his sight, as the soul of a professor; therefore, when he gave us a revelation it could not possibly have been his will that we were required to accept uncritically whatever word it pleased the men of learning to designate as "a Word of God." This type of reasoning caused Luther and our forefathers to insist that they in no way were under any obligation to accept what popes, priests, and professors formally promulgated as Christianity and the Word of God; for they had both the right and the obligation to investigate the facts for themselves, according to their ability. They laughed at the assertion of the papists, that the Bible is the most dangerous of all books when placed within the reach of the uneducated and unordained because it cannot possibly be comprehended aright by lay people, and, moreover, it must be interpreted so as to harmonize with the infallible teachings of the popes. In this matter, as well as in others, the theologians of our day normally react just like real papists: they do allow the common people to read the Bible which, let us face it, is available to all, notwithstanding the murmur of some of the theologians who meticulously emphasize that it is impossible for lay people to understand the Bible. They contend that the Bible cannot possibly be understood without a deep insight into the original languages of the Bible, oriental figurative speech, occidental philosophy, and so forth. Meanwhile, among those who lack all or part of this specialized knowledge, which undeniably includes even a goodly number of the pastors, there are, nevertheless, individual persons who have the desire and need to know which Christianity is truly genuine. Surely, we may well expect that they, like their forefathers, will refuse to allow such objections to deter them from reading the New Testament in their mother tongue; they will quickly discover that whatever legitimate criticism that can be directed against the Christianity of our forefathers, it is, nevertheless, genuine beyond compare to what nowadays is usually offered as such.

As we read the New Testament, we quickly observe that the

historical Jesus Christ is the foundation on which the apostles build and to which they constantly refer as the great warrant for their assertion that what they proclaim is not human wisdom, but the Word of God, that is, a supernaturally revealed, divine wisdom unto salvation; and we encounter this historical Jesus in the four Gospels. It is generally acknowledged among us today that history — especially the story or biography of a single person — is more easily understood than any other kind of writing because we are all acquainted with human nature and the external circumstances attending the human condition. Consequently, even the most curious things that may be told about a human being are not so incomprehensible as to prevent us from being able to judge their significance. Furthermore, the story of Jesus' life is very clearly presented, and his works and the events surrounding them are so plainly and honestly recorded that not even children need to strain themselves, but only marvel at what they read.

It becomes immediately clear to all readers that Jesus was a true human being, born of a woman, but incomparable as a person in this respect: He had no father, except God himself. As a matter of fact, whatever little we read about his human development is confined, on the one side, to whatever is necessary in order to prove his genuine humanity and, on the other side, to awaken the greatest expectations with respect to his mission on earth. Thereupon, there follows seriatim a succession of stories from the time of his baptism until his death. These stories spontaneously impel the most experienced among our elders, as well as the very immature child, to exclaim: I never have heard anything comparable to this for no other person ever has spoken in this manner; and, surely, a person cannot possibly perform such deeds by himself. Finally, we read that he died and was buried, but arose from the grave on the third day. He revealed himself as a spirit; and, yet, appeared before his friends in bodily form of flesh and blood. Afterward, he was caught up by a cloud and received into heaven.

At this point, any comparison between our forefathers' Christianity and the modern version thereof will show that the fathers accepted the historical narrative of Jesus' life as literally true, and it provided for them the very basis for their Christian faith and hope. They declared that Jesus, as a man, was sinless because he did not have an earthly father; also because he performed acts which lie solely within the power of the almighty creator of the world, they stressed the imperative call to faith in his word similar to their faith in God; and because Jesus arose from the grave, those who believe in him have the sure hope that their bodies, likewise, shall be raised transfigured. On the other hand, we observe that, as a rule, those who are intent on expounding the new Christianity completely reject the manifestation of supernatural power in the life of Jesus. Thus, it follows that they hold the view that the written accounts of the life of Jesus are tales about strange happenings or else prose fiction. However, every story about a person's life, words, and accomplishments which cannot be taken literally ceases to be a history—it becomes either didactic fiction or something imagined, all depending upon whether or not the story of Jesus' life is a true history. The minute we assume that it is a work of the imagination, the story's only mark of excellence lies in the amusing way in which the greatest incongruities are lumped together. It is in the very manner that critical, theological scholars have treated the story as a myth; they have sought to explain it by calling attention, in rapid succession, to myths which may have some semblance to the story of Jesus; and there is hardly a single theologian of the new school who does not regard at least some of the gospel stories, as for example, Jesus' supernatural conception and temptation, the turning of water into wine, and the casting out of the evil spirits as myths! However, even though they acknowledge the truth of the historical Jesus or permit the supernatural elements in that history to stand unattacked, they definitely refuse to either base their faith or explain Jesus' and the apostles' words thereon. It necessarily

20

follows, therefore, that they either regard the historical accounts as a myth, or show evidence of a great lack of understanding and reflection. Surely, even children are able to understand that if Jesus were born in a supernatural way without sin, he died completely voluntarily; he actually rose from the dead and ascended both in spirit and body. Therefore, his words must be believed because of his person and deeds. They must be interpreted in the light of the congruity between his person and his whole life and its events.

Therefore, if the New Testament is to determine what constitutes authentic Christianity, it is obvious that the Christianity which some of our theologians profess is untrue. They contend that Jesus was not the singularly extraordinary person with the marvelous powers that the Gospels describe. On the contrary, he was only a human being subject to the very same conditions under which we live, who by the brilliance of his mind and by using his reasoning powers better than most became a truly renowned person, exemplifying a degree of moral excellence difficult to attain. It is not these theologians alone whose Christianity clearly is false; the same holds true of all who figuratively speaking sever the tongue from the mouth, thereby wresting Jesus' words from the context of his life in order to regard his words as anonymous and, thus, subject to whatever interpretation strikes one's fancy. Naturally, they contend, one is not obliged to believe anything beyond that which appears to be reasonable. Indeed, this is a fault of which nearly all of our present-day scholars are culpable in varying degrees. Whenever they speak of the rights of reason in the interpretation of Scriptures and especially as they exercise these rights, one observes quickly that it is not merely a matter of agreeing with the fathers who realized and supposed that animals are not endowed with reason enabling them to read the Bible, and that individuals of limited intelligence hardly can comprehend what they read. They take for granted that the person who interprets the Scriptures has the right to distort the words whenever he finds them exceeding the bounds of reason. This so-called rationalistic interpretation of the Scriptures rests undeniably upon the presupposition that Jesus, in truth, could not have said anything which would seem unreasonable to us. However, if the historical accounts of the Gospels are true, this supposition is utterly absurd. Seeing Jesus' incomprehensible coming into the world and his many inexplicable deeds, it follows that he also must have had many things to say which seemed unreasonable to ordinary people; yet, he spoke with the intent that they, notwithstanding, might believe in his words which neither would nor could deceive anyone.

It is, of course, customary to argue that what is contrary to reason cannot possibly be true. Consequently, one is under the compulsion to reject every idea expressed by Jesus which is contrary to reason, for to do otherwise would imply that Jesus had not spoken the truth but an untruth. However, such an argument is so inconsiderate that it does not require any rebuttal, partly because it would call for complete agreement as to what constitutes reason. Moreover, it would require proof that what reason dictates is the truth before one would be in position either to determine what is contrary to reason, or with justifiable cause label the controversy untruthful. There are two entirely different questions before us: What Jesus has said? and Whether he spoke the impeccable truth? It is readily acknowledged that it would be pathetic if we, in the process of reading, were to employ the method of looking for what we felt the text ought to say rather than what it actually states. Even if the scholars were in agreement on what we understand by human reason and had proven that nothing can be true which contradicts reason, it could, nevertheless, not have the slightest influence on the interpretation of Jesus' words. Even if his words, according to the meaning of their own linguistic form, did seem absurd, we still would not be entitled to give, contrive, or force another interpretation upon them; rather we should have to draw the conclusion: that either Jesus did not talk sense, or we simply do not know what he said. In both instances, the historical accounts of the Gospels would be a myth. If that which is contrary to reason is equivalent to being untrue, then Jesus, whom the evangelists write about, was not capable of speaking irrationally. Moreover, if their account of Jesus' words is not trustworthy, what are we to make or say about their reports about his mighty works? For according to the testimony of the evangelists, the deeds were performed in order that we might believe his word. Obviously, this is impossible, unless we know what he said. The problem concerning the truth and the trustworthiness of that which Jesus and Christianity declare constitutes, indeed, a distinct subject of inquiry which we, however, must not permit to overshadow the question of the meaning of Jesus' words and the meaning or significance of what we call the true, that is, authentic Christianity. Here, we cannot play with words as if what constitutes true Christianity would depend upon what we assert to be the truth. Such action might, except for the importance of the question, be appropriate in one of Holberg's comedies, but not in scientific investigation. Besides, if being reasonable carries the notion that everything opposite to it ipso facto is a lie, it follows that neither should we attribute reasonableness to anything, except that which is undeniable, that is, cannot be refuted without thereby being affirmed. The self-evident truth, which must be emphasized at this point, is that the people who have declared hundreds of propositions reasonable without proving whether even half of them are undeniable, are the same people who, despite this, unhesitatingly assert that whatever contradicts any of these unproven fundamental propositions is untrue and impossible.

In my reflection on these things, I presuppose that every person who is seriously intent upon studying the New Testament in order to learn what constitutes authentic Christianity also will read Jesus' own sayings; supposing that he does this, it surely will become clearer and clearer to him each moment that, according to the New Testament, the Christianity of our time is altogether false and, on the contrary, that of our Lutheran forefathers is wholly genuine. Although pointing to the New Testament may be a futile effort in the case of the person who neither considers it important to read the New Testament with a reflective mind nor to read it more than once, I shall, nevertheless, cite several of Jesus' sayings about his own identity, his mission, and his church which, even if they serve no other purpose will, nevertheless, make my thoughts clear.

It is common knowledge that Jesus called himself both the Son of God and the Son of man. Whenever we read the story of his origin as a real and true history, we cannot, even for a moment, doubt—regardless of whatever these words may imply—but that he thereby wanted, among other things, to remind his hearers that he on the side of his Father was the Son of God, and on the side of his Mother the Son of man; he shared the Spirit in common with God, and body and heart in common with us.

Yes, Jesus, who called himself the only begotten Son of God and accomplished, according to the evangelists' report, truly divine acts, says,

> The Son can do nothing on his own account, but only what he sees the Father doing; for whatsoever he does, that the Son does likewise. . . . For as the Father raises the dead and gives them life, so also the Son gives life to whom he will. The Father judges no one, but has given all judgment to the Son, that all may honor the Son, even as they honor the Father. (John 5:19, 21, 22, 23a) All things have been delivered to me by my Father; and no one knows the Son except the Father, and no one knows the Father except the Son and any one to whom the Son chooses to reveal him. (Matt. 11:27) The Father knows me and I know the Father. . . . I and the Father are one. (John 10:15, 30) The Father is in me and I am in the Father. (John 10:38b) He who has seen me has seen the Father. . . . Believe me that I am in the Father and the Father in me; or else believe me for the sake of the works themselves. . . . Whatever you ask in my name, I will do it, that the Father may be glorified in the Son. . . . Father glorify thou me in thy own presence with the glory which I had with thee before the world was made! (John 14:9, 11, 13; 17:5)

Consider this Jesus who, without an earthly father, was conceived in his mother's womb by the Spirit of God, and how he, with a single word, commanded the powers of nature and raised the dead. Reflecting on the manner in which he speaks about himself and his relationship to the Father, who is God, is it thinkable that any rational reader will conclude that Jesus thereby intended to say that he in reality was not different from any other individual, except more virtuous and wiser than the rank and file of people? He spoke in this manner in order to emphasize that he was not only greater than all the scribes who wanted to criticize him, but even superior to the prophets who prophesied about him. In the name of the Lord, he performed marvelous signs and works among the people.

Here, indeed, the truthful and reflective reader will discover unquestionably that, according to Jesus' own words, his disciples, yes, all Christians, are impelled by faith to acknowledge his divinity, even though this oneness with the Father admittedly is too deep a mystery for man to fathom. Nevertheless, the testimony of this divinely magnificent relationship together with the accounts of his mighty works shall be proclaimed among all generations of people who bear the name "Christian" after him and place their hope of eternal bliss in his words. This will become increasingly clear as we read and reflect upon Christ's words concerning his mission among us and his church.

There is no basis for any reasonable person to doubt that the only begotten Son, who manifested the glory given to him by the Father before the creation of the world, had an earthly ministry which no one else could have accomplished; therefore, he allowed himself to be born as a man and subjected himself to be tempted, afflicted, tortured, and, finally, executed as a despised and rejected person. Whosoever views Jesus' ministry merely as a ministry which even John the Baptist might have been capable of undertaking either does not know what he is saying, or he is saying, in effect, that he believes neither the history of Jesus nor his words about his eternal glory with God (cf. John 8:54; 17:22, 24). It does not require proof to see that their interpretation of Christianity is completely false, if according to their assertion,

Jesus' ministry was solely that of teaching the people, slightly better than Gamaliel but far below that of every other contemporary German professor of natural religion. Besides, it may well be in order to keep in mind that the view of those who regard Jesus' teaching and personal example as his chief ministry conflicts both with his words and the historical account of his life.

Jesus says,

> For this is the will of my Father, that every one who sees the Son and believes in him should have eternal life; and I will raise him up at the last day. . . . I am the living bread which comes down from heaven, that a man may eat of it and not die. I am the living bread which came down from heaven; if any one eats of this bread, he will live for ever; and the bread which I shall give for the life of the world is my flesh. . . . I am the good shepherd. The good shepherd lays down his life for the sheep. . . . I lay down my life for the sheep. . . . I lay down my life, that I may take it again. No one takes it from me, but I lay it down of my own accord. I have power to lay it down, and I have power to take it again; . . . For God so loved the world that he gave his only Son, that whoever believes in him should not perish but have eternal life. . . . I did not come to judge the world but to save the world. (John 6:40, 51; 10:11, 15; 18:17, 18; 3:16; 12:47) For the Son of man came to seek and to save the lost. (Luke 19:10) The Son of man came not to be served but to serve, and to give his life as a ransom for many. (Matt. 20:28) Truly, truly, I say to you, unless a grain of wheat falls into the earth and dies, it remains alone; but if it dies, it bears fruit. (John 12:24) Shall I not drink the cup which the Father has given me? (John 18:11)

What here instantly becomes apparent is that Jesus constantly testifies that the purpose of his coming is that all might believe in him and thus obtain eternal life—everlasting salvation. From this it is obvious, indeed, that Jesus came to remove every obstacle or to fulfill the condition for man's salvation which could not be met by teaching alone. If the condition for salvation could have been met through teaching, the sending of a prophet would have been sufficient; and John the Baptist, above all others, would have been qualified for there would have been no need to prepare the way for another. Neither can it escape our attention that Jesus here emphatically gives great weight to his death as real self-sacrifice which no one else can make, except he who has life in himself and power to lay it down and to take it again. Regardless of how incomprehensible the reason for such self-sacrifice necessarily must be, Jesus' own words make it clear as day that the sacrifice was inevitable; if it were necessary for the Son of God to suffer physical death for our salvation, we realize quickly that he had to have been born as a true human being and that neither a prophet nor an angel from heaven could accomplish his mission. Moreover, that the Son of God, whose coming among us was inevitable, also appeared as a teacher of divine truths and gave an incomparable testimony concerning heavenly and spiritual things is something that we are bound to recognize as being natural and proper. Even though we may fail altogether in perceiving how his chief mission of self-sacrifice encompassed his whole life as well as his death, there never can be any doubt but that his life had to be the very mirror of divine life in human form, pure and unblemished.

At this point, there may perhaps be those who find reason to question whether our Lutheran forefathers in their pondering upon the mystery of the power and efficacy of Jesus' death adhered strictly to Jesus' words which speak exclusively of his death as the condition for sinful human beings' salvation and inheritance of eternal life, or whether they, possibly on the basis of their own premises, one-sidedly viewed Jesus' death as the all-comprehensive act of redemption. However, there never can be any doubt but that it would be contrary to Jesus' words if we, conjointly with our present-day scholars, were to view Jesus' death as similar to that of any other God-fearing person who testified with his blood that he believed and so he spoke (cf. 2 Cor. 4:13), for surely the death of the Son of God necessarily implied a purpose which could not be accomplished through the death of any other human being. Jesus identifies this purpose by comparing himself to a grain of wheat which must die in order to bear much fruit (John 12:24); he also declares that his flesh is

27

given "for the life of the world," as well as "a ransom for many" (John 6:51; Mark 10:45), and that his blood is to be poured out "for many for the forgiveness of sins" (Matt. 26:28). Therefore, when the scholars say that the death of Jesus is only intended to be a pledge of God's willingness to forgive us our sins, what they are thus saying really does not convey even the least intelligible meaning, since the death of Jesus is not seen as the condition for the forgiveness of sin. If this is not the case, there is no way in which his death, Jesus' own words notwithstanding, could include any payment or basis for salvation in itself; at most it would be a pledge that Jesus believed that God would be gracious toward us, but by that one presupposes that Jesus was no different from us — only a human being. However, if he were the Son of God, he undeniably could give us a pledge far more certain than the ambiguous meaning of death as the pledge of God's grace, which he not only believed but embodied in himself. As an example of such a pledge, drawn from among others, there is the case of the paralytic where Jesus proved that "the Son of man has power on earth to forgive sins" (Matt. 9:2–6). Indeed, the necessity for the death of Jesus, the Son of God, and the saving power of his death are undeniable, according to Jesus' words. Therefore, whosoever denies these things (i.e., his self-disclosures) rejects, in effect, that the Son of man was the Son of God — perfect in his wisdom, truthful in his speech, and powerfully able to forgive sinners; and such a person does not, in any manner, belong to those whom Jesus calls his disciples, his sheep, his flock, his servants, his kingdom, and his church.

Now, if Jesus' words about his divine glory and his unique mission on earth show that it was imperative for him that people believed he was the only begotten Son of God and mankind's indispensable Savior who by his self-sacrifice obtained the forgiveness of sin and eternal life for all who willingly believe, one readily discerns that the Christianity which our Lutheran forefathers confessed was, according to the New Testament, completely genuine, whereas the new Christianity, which contradicts the old, is completely false. In the case of those who still are uncertain about what Jesus meant by "believing on him," his words to and about the believers ought to clarify the matter.

Even as Jesus categorically declares that "He who believes in him is not condemned; he who does not believe is condemned already, because he has not believed in the name of the only Son of God" (John 3:18), in like manner, he repeatedly emphasizes that whoever seeks his help must not only believe he is able to help, but unashamedly confess his faith in him. For Christ says,

> So every one who acknowledges me before men, I also will acknowledge before my Father who is in heaven (Matt. 10:32, 33) He who loves father or mother more than me is not worthy of me; and he who does not take his cross and follow me is not worthy of me. (Matt. 10:37, 38) If any man would come after me, let him deny himself and take up his cross and follow me. For whoever would save his life will lose it, and whoever loses his life for my sake will find it. (Matt. 16:24, 25)

Surely none can fail to perceive that when Jesus speaks about having faith in him, in no way does he limit his understanding thereof to the obligation of accepting his teaching. It goes further, for it implies the obligation to submit oneself to him in loving and unrestrained trust and unashamedly acknowledge this loyalty before the world, even though such a step may split the strongest human ties which bind us to what we value dearest on earth: parents, children, and our common life in this world. This is precisely what our Lutheran forefathers taught, and they appropriated, on behalf of the entire church, the words of the apostle Peter:

> Lord, to whom shall we go? You have the words of eternal life; and we believe, and have come to know, that you are the Holy One of God. (John 6:68, 69) You are the Christ, the Son of the living God. And Jesus answered him, "Blessed are you, Simon Bar-Jona! For flesh and blood has not revealed this to you, but my Father who is in heaven. And I tell you, you are Peter, and on this rock I will build my church, and the powers of death shall not prevail against it." (Matt. 16:16–18)

On the basis of the New Testament, it is hard to see how their Christianity can be considered genuine when they reduce faith in Jesus Christ to absolute nothingness by defining faith merely as recognizing Jesus as a divine teacher and assenting to his teaching, because they find it to be in agreement with reason; indeed, a position which freely allows them to refute his divine power and glory, the power of his death, and the prerequisite of faith in his name and person as the condition for salvation. Apparently, this makes it perfectly possible for an individual to believe in him while, at the same time, not merely questioning, but denying and refuting that Jesus demands that his disciples believe in him — yes, requires that they steadfastly confess their faith and, if necessary, seal their confession with their blood rather than suffer loss of his friendship and their salvation. Still, our present-day theologians are usually not even satisfied with surreptitiously designating themselves as the true, reasonable, unprejudiced, and enlightened Christians despite their denial of the substance of the faith and its saving power. Thus, this very denial and refutation, they insist, warrants their claim to be regarded as true Christians.

Therefore, any one who resolutely confesses and earnestly defends the faith — that Jesus Christ is the divine Savior, full of power and glory, to whom we must submit ourselves and renounce the world if we are to obtain salvation — such a person, in their view, is in no way to be regarded as a Christian, but rather to be seen as an un-Christian, unreasonable, and misanthropic fanatic. Under such circumstances, it is easy to see that the question to be resolved is: Who shall be labeled un-Christian? Those who believe and confess what Christ expects to be believed and confessed in his church, or those who deny, fight, and blaspheme this faith?

When Jesus demands a total commitment on the part of those who believe in him, and, moreover, requires acts of self-denial and self-sacrifice, both prompted by love and done for his sake and in his name, it is quite obvious that, according to his word, he and his church must be seen as constituting a spiritual and genuine unity. For this very reason, every Christian's life must become one in communion with the Savior through faith and love which, in turn, inevitably results in a similar mutuality among the believers. Consequently, it is quite obvious that if two can become one with a third and the three experience a sense of oneness, the same holds true regardless of how large a number of persons one may mention, or how multiple their diversity. This is the conclusion to which our Lutheran forefathers correctly were led; yet, perhaps they failed somewhat to give appropriate weight to the living unity in Christ which, according to his words, is inseparable from sharing in his self-sacrifice and in the forgiveness of sin and salvation which he thereby won for his adherents. Our present-day scholars, on the contrary, tend to reject every word about this spiritual unity with the Savior—rooted in faith and love—on the basis that such words are expressive of a crude, sensate, and wholly unbiblical mysticism; and how little they care about Jesus' own words is at no time more clearly evident than here. Yet, there is no teaching which Jesus has uttered more clearly and emphatically underscored. He not only presupposes this oneness by demanding self-sacrifice in his name, which is unthinkable apart from this selfsame oneness, but he says,

Truly, truly, I say to you, unless you eat the flesh of the Son of man and drink of his blood, you have no life in you; he who eats my flesh and drinks my blood has eternal life, and I will raise him up at the last day. For my flesh is food indeed, and my blood is drink indeed. He who eats my flesh and drinks my blood abides in me, and I in him. As the living Father sent me, and I live because of the Father, so he who eats me will live because of me. (John 6:53–57)

I am the true vine, and my Father is the vinedresser. Every branch of mine that bears no fruit, he takes away, and every branch that does bear fruit, he prunes that it may bear more fruit. . . . Abide in me, and I in you. As the branch cannot bear fruit by itself, unless it abides in the vine, neither can you, unless you abide in me. I am the vine, you are the branches. He who abides in me, and I in him, he it is that bears much fruit, for apart from me you can do nothing. If a man does not abide in me, he is cast forth as a branch and withers; and the branches are gathered, thrown into the fire and burned. (John 15:1–2, 4–6)

And for their sake I consecrate myself, that they also may be consecrated in truth. I do not pray for these only, but also for those who are to believe in me through their word, that they may all be one, even as thou, Father, art in me, and I in thee, that they also may be in us, so that the world may believe that thou hast sent me. The glory which thou hast given me I have given to them, that they may be one even as we are one, I in them and thou in me, that they may become perfectly one, so that the world may know that thou hast sent me and hast loved them even as thou hast loved me. (John 17:19–23)

If a man loves me, he will keep my word, and my Father will love him, and we will come and make our home with him. (John 14:23)

The scholars now tell us that this unity, which Jesus so vigorously dwells on, is not the sort of unity that demands the believers' heartfelt and unreserved submission to the Savior, coupled with self-sacrifice on their part, because it is not an intrinsic but only a moral union. In so doing, they clearly make known: first, that despite Jesus' word, they deny his real and essential oneness with the Father on the grounds that we, too, according to the explicit words of Jesus, shall be one with him, even as he and the Father are one; secondly, despite Jesus' word, they refuse to know anything about his self-sacrifice as the very foundation and condition of our salvation; and, finally, they either do not mean or do not know what they themselves are saying. For what constitutes moral unity, unless several persons, thereby, bring about the integrated moral individual? Moreover, if we are one in Christ also as moral individuals, it follows that his morality is ours, and ours likewise is his. It can hardly be believed that they mean to say that such a moral unity can be effected between essentially diverse persons, or be brought about between Jesus and us without mutual self-denial in faith and love. Hence, if the proponents of the new Christianity are in basic agreement with our Lutheran forefathers, except for certain unbiblical statements which offend them, they should cease characterizing the forefathers' Christianity as a superstition; likewise, they ought to cease branding those descendants of the fathers who share their views as obscurants, mystics, and fanatics, or else they plainly contradict and reject Jesus' own words and teaching. Yes, they attribute to Jesus Christ and to us and our forefathers superstition, obscurantism, crass mysticism, and furious fanaticism. Surely, if such be the case, it would hardly seem proper and surely would be unpleasant for them to bear the name Christian after such an unenlightened visionary and fanatic mystic.

Examining the *Third Article: Of the Son of God* which, of course, must be the chief article of the Christian religion, we discover that the teaching of our Lutheran forefathers was in full agreement with Jesus' own words as recorded in the New Testament. Naturally, those who protest against the Augsburg Confession also protest against the validity of the gospel history and the words of Christ recorded therein. Consequently, it becomes impossible for any thoughtful reader of the New Testament to turn to them in his or her search for the meaning of Christianity if its very message, as the protesters contend, must be Christ's own teaching preserved and passed on to us through the New Testament. Martin Luther and our forefathers jointly asserted that whoever gets at the truth of the article concerning Christ—his person, his mission, and relationship to the believing church—is not in any serious danger of failing to comprehend what else belongs to Christianity for the simple reason that everything essential to Christianity is included and narrowed down into this chief article. Those who favored the papacy protested, to be sure, on the very valid grounds that they did not find a single word in this article concerning Christ about the pope and all the letters of indulgence and good works which he had in his power to distribute freely or to sell. Nevertheless, Luther was undeniably correct in saying that when inquiring about Christianity, one is not asking about the papacy, and that if anyone claims to be the vicar of Christ on earth he is obliged to present his credentials, signed by Christ himself; moreover, he is duty-bound neither to subtract from nor to add to what Christ has declared to be the truth that leads to salvation. Rather, his task is to teach and affirm this truth, for nothing can be subtracted from Christ's teaching without making it a lie. And nothing can be added without declaring that his words of eternal life either are incomplete or inadequate, which is equivalent to saying they are not the words of eternal life or that the eternal life is insufficient for us. In this very same manner, our rationalistic scholars with their reverence for reason protest against the article concerning Christ. They object to this chief article of the Christian religion because it does not contain a single word about the merits of reason and its inherent potential for shedding light on divine things; furthermore, the article does not say anything about all the moral virtues and heroic acts which reason is capable of effecting by itself, thereby bringing about every possible kind of happiness. Also, it is very true that neither Christ nor the gospel writers utter a single word about these things. However, as Christians we have the undeniable right and responsibility to reply. Regardless of how providential all these things appear to be — the role of reason in enlightening the mind and in performing deeds of virtue and heroic acts — none of these belong intrinsically to Christianity, for neither Christ nor the gospel writers speak thereof. Thus, we can no more recognize reason than the pope in Rome as the vicar of Christ, unless they (i.e., the rationalists) present credentials, signed by Christ himself, and tenaciously cling to Christ as the Word of eternal life, from whose words nothing must be subtracted or added.

2

The Augsburg Confession

In any comprehensive study of our forefathers' Christianity, we turn, as everyone knows, to the Augsburg Confession which constitutes an equally excellent and indispensable source material. Here, besides the fundamental article concerning Jesus Christ, we come upon three distinctive tenets: concerning the Trinity, justification, and the means of grace; all of which are a plague to our rationalistic theologians who declare that these tenets are equally un-Christian, unbiblical, and unreasonable. It is possible that there may be far more truth in this assertion than these supercilious gentlemen envision. For if, as they claim, the Logos is divine reason and Jesus, as the Gospel testifies, is the Christ, it is obviously most reasonable to believe in Jesus and take him, as divine reason, at his word. Therefore, if these teachings are rooted in his words, they are as reasonable, indeed, as they are biblical and Christian. Since it is commonly known that it is merely an empty compliment whenever the rationalists call Jesus divine reason or call him the Son of God, our Lord, we shall here simply let the question of the reasonableness of our forefathers' teaching stand on its own merit, and simply limit our investigation to the principal issue: Whether, in the light of the New Testament, their professed Christianity was authentic and genuine?

First of all, with respect to the Trinity, we already have made reference to Christ's testimony concerning the Son's personal differentiation from and yet essential unity with the Father (cf. John 5, 14). Hence, the only question here becomes that of the personality of the Holy Spirit and his relationship to the Father and the Son, namely: Are there, according to Jesus' testimony, three or two coequal persons in the godhead?

In the first place, when the Holy Spirit is referred to as a divine person in the Gospels, we are obliged to agree on the ground that the Gospels expressly state that at the baptism of Jesus, the Holy Spirit appeared in a recognizable and bodily form (Matt. 3:13–17; Mark 1:9–12; Luke 3:21–22; John 1:29–34). Surely, one must be a person in order to show oneself in a distinct, bodily form. Far from contradicting this concept, Jesus' words most clearly support this idea, and attribute divine personality to the Holy Spirit; this is as axiomatic as his words to the Apostles: "Go therefore and make disciples of all nations, baptizing them in the name of the Father and of the Son and of the Holy Spirit" (Matt. 28:19). Whosoever is expected to possess the qualities that correspond to his name must at least be a person, and if that person's name deserves to be placed next to the name of God, he undeniably must be on equality with God. Thus, we face an alternative: either Jesus hereby wanted to say that there are three gods or that there is a threeness in the one divine godhead. We know that Jesus in the clearest language possible spoke about the oneness of God; we also know that he traced the divine nature of the Son to his oneness with the Father; and finally, he definitely made it known that the Holy Spirit, who comes from the Father, is divinely one with the Father and the Son. Specifically, Jesus says:

> When they deliver you up, do not be anxious how you are to speak or what you are to say; for what you are to say will be given to you in that hour; for it is not you who speak, but the Spirit of your Father speaking through you. (Matt. 10:19, 20)
> And I will pray the Father, and will give you another Counselor,

to be with you for ever, even the Spirit of truth, whom the world cannot receive, because it neither sees him nor knows him; you know him, for he dwells with you, and will be in you. (John 14:16, 17)

In that day you will know that I am in my Father, and you in me, and I in you . . . but the Counselor, the Holy Spirit, whom the Father will send in my name, he will teach you all things, and bring to your remembrance all that I have said to you. (John 14:20, 26)

When the Counselor comes, whom I shall send to you from the Father, even the Spirit of truth, who proceeds from the Father, he will bear witness to me, and you also are witnesses, because you have been with me from the beginning. (John 15:26, 27)

I have yet many things to say to you, but you cannot bear them now. When the Spirit of truth comes, he will guide you into all the truth; for he will not speak on his own authority, but whatever he hears he will speak, and he will declare to you the things that are to come. He will glorify me, for he will take what is mine and declare it to you. All that the Father has is mine; therefore I said that he will take what is mine and declare it to you. (John 16:12–15)

Frankly, I would not think very highly of the intelligence of any individual human being who could fail to see that Jesus here speaks of the Holy Spirit as a real person, similar to the personality of the Father and the Son. The Holy Spirit acts on his own. However, like the Son, he does not speak on his own authority for he is not only the Spirit of the Father, but also of the Son. The latter is self-evident, for it is the Son who is charged with sending the Spirit of truth (cf. John 14:25, 26; 15:26, 27). According to Jesus' self-disclosure, the Son has the truth in himself by virtue of being the Son of God. He testifies, "I am . . . the truth" (John 14:6).

Therefore, the question is not what Greek, Roman, French, German, or Danish pagans either have understood or do understand about "spirit" and God's spirit, but what shall we, in the light of Jesus' own words, think and believe about the Holy Spirit as the Spirit of God and of truth? This is definitely the only question that can be asked, for I am of the opinion that one must be preposterously stupid in order to doubt whose teaching concerning the Holy Spirit is the correct Christian position: either our Lutheran forefathers or our present-day scholars. The forefathers regarded and honored the Holy Spirit as God's all-powerful and all-knowing representative in God's new kingdom on earth, constantly at work in Christ's church and congregation. Contrarily, our present-day scholars view the Holy Spirit as wholly impersonal, indeterminate, and unconcious, in effect, a nonentity. In one instance they apply an empty name to divine power and wisdom, in another to Christianity, and in still another to the Christian frame of mind. Obviously, according to this view the Holy Spirit cannot reach beyond our own reason; for if the Holy Spirit is not the divine means creating the divine and living bond between God and us, there simply is no other way whereby God can have a spiritual effect upon us. Thus, there is no other spiritual bond between either God or Christ and us than what we commonly call our own reason. This is, of course, the general position of the scholars who insist that any divine work accomplished in us, except through reason, is, nonetheless, physical in essence regardless of how great we adjudge its spiritual effect upon us. Consequently, it is fantastic and preposterous in their opinion. In other words, if our scholars' notions about the Holy Spirit were to be considered Christian, then it must have been Jesus' intention that we should baptize in the name of reason; and our own reason would constitute the divine Advocate from and of the Father—the interpreter of Jesus's words and guide to the full truth—whom Jesus promised to send to his disciples (cf. John 14:26, 15:13–15; 16:13). As many have been expected, it became customary to believe that blasphemy against the Son of man was far less serious than any derision of our own reason, for in this life, at least, such action is unforgivable. Without discussing here all the other difficulties inherent in such an interpretation of Jesus' words—which might more rightly be called a "misinterpretation"—I will simply point out that his "divine" reason, promised by Jesus and bestowed by the Father, in the name of Jesus, upon those who believed on the Son and by which we are to be baptized, undeniably must be regarded as a "new" reason which, in effect, belongs exclusively to the Christians. Therefore, there is no way in which this "new" reason can be regarded as synonymous with that reason which the ancient, pagan Greeks and Romans displayed; similarly, we cannot identify this "new" reason with that of those among us who neither have faith in Jesus nor have received Christian baptism. Nevertheless, the scholars insist that the reason of which they speak is by no means dependent upon faith in Jesus. Moreover, it definitely is not a gift of Christ bestowed in baptism upon those who believe in him, but rather the very same reason which the wise pagans possessed and venerated; yes, the very court before which the question whether we must believe in Jesus and to what extent we are able to build upon his words is to be decided. Thus, it is quite obvious that that spirit and reason which our scholars declare to be the only true interpreter and mankind's only spiritual guide to the full truth cannot possibly be identified with the Holy Spirit, because Jesus' promise to his disciples was not fulfilled until after his glorification. The apostles received the Holy Spirit when Jesus, after his resurrection, breathed upon them and on the Day of Pentecost when they received power from above. That Jesus here could not possibly have intended either to identify the Holy Spirit with his own teaching or with that mode of thought which came to characterize those who followed it does not require any proof, because according to Jesus' words the Holy Spirit knows who he is and what to say. Viewed in this manner, it undeniably follows that the Holy Spirit, as Jesus declares, will not speak of himself. On the contrary, he will utter what he hears and will address himself, through the apostles, about things which they themselves never had thought about, and in this way the Holy Spirit will be seen by us in the very same personal light as the Father and the Son.

When viewed in the light of Jesus' words, our Lutheran forefathers' teaching about the Holy Spirit—that is, about the Trinity—is genuinely Christian, whereas that of our present-day scholars is manifestly false. Despite the fact that our fore-fathers at times may have stated some unbiblical views about this mystery and thus failed to adhere strictly to those words of Jesus which show the relationship between the Father, Son, and Holy Spirit; yet, they never forgot that the Father is as the very name signifies, the sources of all divinity. Thus, the emphasis which they placed upon the divine nature of the Son and of the Holy Spirit was thoroughly Christian. Indeed, the words of Jesus declare that it is the will of the Father that mankind's full and eternal salvation shall be accomplished by the Son and the Holy Spirit who, therefore, in order to accomplish this divine mission and perform God's work in us and for us, necessarily must possess divine power and wisdom and share alike in the honor which we give the Father. Regardless of how absurd and unreasonable the doctrine of the Trinity might appear, it is, nonetheless, according to Jesus' words, fundamentally Christian, and, according to the faith, the very source of all true and living Christianity on earth. Even if someone were able to prove the impossibility of the Trinity, he would not thereby have proven that Christianity is a false teaching which no human being ought to believe and follow. However, our chief concern here lies exclusively in discovering what, according to the New Testament, constitutes true Christianity. Wherefore, we shall not involve ourselves in any investigation of the truth of Christianity, for such an inquiry ought to be undertaken entirely on its own. Any attempt to give a reasonable answer to this question is simply impossible unless we first know what Christianity actually is. To investigate whether something—one does not know what—is true is undeniably equivalent to investigating whether everything unknown is true, and that, as a matter of course, is simply to beat the air. It is only because we are so accustomed to hearing the advocates of the impossibility of the Trinity discuss this question in such a way as if it already were decided that I here wish to indicate: first, we are not speaking about three physical bodies, but about three spiritual beings; second, if it be impossible for three to share equally in the one godhead, how much less probable is it that countless millions of human beings could share a common humanity? Those who say that the one and same qualities of nature and reason belong to all of us speak at least a thousand times less rationally than we who say that the deity of the Father, Son, and Holy Spirit is one and the same!

Today, we not only hear people declaring with almost unanimous voice that our forefathers' teaching about the Trinity is totally un-Christian, unbelievable, and contrary to reason, but they even more strongly reject and bitterly deride our forefathers' teaching about justification by God's grace—wholly unmerited—through faith in Jesus Christ. Concerning this teaching and the pertinent articles about man's natural sinfulness and lack of power to turn to the good, they contend that these teachings are not only unreasonable but morally depriving because, on the one side, they serve to disguise the utterly profligate persons, and, on the other side, they deprive the individual human being of faith in his own power to bring about moral self-improvement.

The task before us is neither to investigate whether the concern for developing morality lies closer to the heart of our contemporary exponents of moral philosophy than to Martin Luther, nor to inquire whether present-day moral theories deserve the criticism and ridicule to which they have been and still are subjected day by day. Succinctly stated, the question before us is whether the teaching, according to the New Testament, is Christian? If the answer is affirmative, the rationalists will have to decide with Christ whether or not his teaching is morally harmful.

Surely, it requires only good vision to observe that according to the Gospels, there is full agreement between Jesus Christ and Martin Luther with respect to the faith in God's only begotten

Son who alone is able to save mankind from perdition and make us blessed. Further, even the repent and unbelieving, not to mention the ungodly and unbelieving, are by themselves wholly unable, apart from Jesus, to accomplish what is good. Since the scholars, nonetheless, persistently maintain that Christ is on their side and that the Lutheran teaching on the subject of justification is at the very best Pauline but in no way Christian, it surely behooves us once more to listen to what Jesus says.

We have no desire whatsoever to engage in controversy with anyone on such questions as to whether all human beings are sinners, how this happened, and what is the meaning of justification. Here, we find no definitive utterances of Jesus. Hence, we are obliged to adhere to the main issue which undeniably is whether we, according to Jesus' words, can obtain salvation without acknowledging that we are sinners, and second, whether we by ourselves — apart from Christ and apart from the Spirit bestowed upon us in Christ's name — are able to do what is good and acceptable to the Father. This is indisputably the main issue. For if our redemption, according to Jesus' words, is effected solely by the Father's love revealed through the Son and the Spirit, and if we all stand in need of the forgiveness of sin and eternal life which are granted to us by the Son of God, our Savior, by virtue of his self-sacrifice and our faith in his redeeming power, then our forefathers' teaching was fundamentally Christian, according to Jesus' words. The position of the rationalists, on the contrary, that human beings do not stand in need of forgiveness (or if they do, it can be gained through personal remorsefulness and uprightness) and that we will become blessed by virtue of our moral excellence is totally un-Christian.

In what has preceded heretofore, we already have seen that if Jesus were not the only begotten Son of God, he would have had to be the greatest deceiver and the most arrogant fanatic under the sun. The same would be true if neither his incarnation nor his death were inexorably necessary for the salvation and eternal life of all people, and if our union with him through faith and love were not the only way to a godly and blessed life. Here, even at the risk of redundancy, we append the following: Jesus preached and said,

> Repent, and believe in the gospel. (Mark 1:15) Those who are well have no need of a physician, but those who are sick; I have not come to call the righteous, but sinners to repentance. (Luke 5:31–32) For the Son of man came to seek and to save that which was lost. (Luke 19:10) He who believes in him is not condemned; he who does not believe is condemned already, because he has not believed in the name of the only Son of God. And this is the judgment, that the light has come into the world, and men loved darkness rather than light, because their deeds were evil. (John 3:18–19) While you have the light, believe in the light, that you may become sons of light. (John 12:36) I am the light of the world; he who follows me will not walk in darkness, but will have the light of life. (John 8:12) I am the way, and the truth, and the life; no one comes to the Father, but by me. (John 14:6) I am the door; if any one enters by me, he will be saved, and will go in and out and find pasture. (John 10:9) My sheep hear my voice, and I know them, and they follow me; and I give them eternal life. (John 10:27–28) I am the resurrection and the life; he who believes in me, though he die, yet shall he live, and whoever lives and believes in me shall never die. (John 11:25–26)

When Jesus asks for repentance on the part of all those whom he calls and declares that only sinners stand in need of repentance, it cannot be disputed that he regards all of them as sinners. Moreover, when he asserts that faith is the one and only means of escape from divine judgment, he is clearly saying, that it is by faith alone that we are justified—understanding justification as the divine pardon by which we are set free from judgment. When Jesus definitely places himself between God and all human beings as the spiritual light and life which by faith alone may become ours, he unequivocally excludes, even from among those who believe in him, any idea of having gained meritoriousness. On the contrary, some may take exception and maintain that, even without spiritual life and light, it is possible to accomplish things marked by spiritual quality. However, according to Jesus' words, we dare not say that there might be some righteous people on the earth who neither need repentance nor faith in him, nor light and life from him. Even if someone should contemplate taking such a view, Jesus declares that "he who is not with me is against me" (Matt. 12:30). "If a man does not abide in me, he is cast forth as a branch and withers" (John 15:6). As for those who deem themselves to be righteous, he says that they "are like whitewashed tombs, which outwardly appear beautiful, but within are full of dead men's bones and all uncleanness" (Matt. 23:27–28).

Were there actually other sayings of Jesus which, contradicting those quoted above, claimed either that one could obtain eternal bliss apart from faith in Jesus or accomplish that which is good without him, these would prove, indeed, that Jesus in his guidance concerning the way of salvation obviously had contradicted himself and thus demonstrated that he, in his own person, was not the light and the truth. Nothing could be more unfortunate than to argue about his teaching, for whosoever teaches two definitely contradictory views as the truth is, as a matter of fact, not teaching anything, except, perhaps, his own standpoint—that "yes" and "no," and "truth" and "falsehood" are one and the same. In such a situation we really would not need any teacher, regardless of how much we do need him. Therefore, whosoever is intent upon insisting that, according to Jesus' words, it is Christian to believe we can both perform good works and be saved without faith in him and without spiritual union with him, will have to concede that, according to Jesus' words, the very opposite is also Christian. Thus, this individual must either draw the conclusion that Christianity is sheer falsehood or deceit, or that by the approval and extolment of such teaching to the level of a divine revelation concerning the truth of salvation, he labels himself as either a maniac or a deceiver.

However, Jesus, according to his own words, was definitely not among those who think that "yes" and "no" can be placed in juxtaposition. On the contrary, we hear him solemnly affirming, "He who is not with me is against me, and he who does not gather with me scatters" (Matt. 12:30). Moreover, he drew the sharpest line of separation between himself, as the Son of God, and his enemies, the children of the devil — yes, between himself, as the truth, and the devil, as the liar and that father of lies, in whom there is no truth. He emphatically declares, "No one can serve two masters" (Matt. 6:24), and "No city or house divided against itself will stand" (Matt. 12:25b). Indeed, it is next to impossible to presume such gross self-contradiction on the part of a teacher as clear-thinking as Jesus. Hence, his enemies actually have failed, despite many centuries, to ensnare him in his speech. Consequently, when those who allege to be his friends insist that they now have succeeded in discovering sayings of Jesus which make his above-printed words a lie, they stamp not only his words, but also the Christianity which all the past generations built upon his words as a lie. This is an assertion, indeed, which is incredibly hard to believe, for who can possibly be less trustworthy than those who make Jesus out to be a liar while doing themselves the honor of being called his friends, disciples, and true imitators!

However, when we listen to what these supposedly wise gentlemen have to say about those specific words whereby Jesus, according to their judgement, is supposed to have contradicted himself, it immediately becomes clear that what we are hearing are only frivolous utterances. Who can seriously believe that Jesus in his reply to the lawyer, who sought to trap Jesus by asking him about the greatest commandment in the law, weakens, even the least, in his teaching about the natural weakness of human beings and the necessity for faith? Speaking to the lawyer, Jesus says, "You have answered right; do this" — love God with your whole being, and your neighbor as yourself — "and you will live" (Luke 10:28). Moreover, they point to Jesus' words in which he assures us that "not every one who says to me, 'Lord, Lord,' shall enter the kingdom of heaven, but he who does the will of my Father who is in heaven" (Matt. 7:21). Indeed, it takes a considerable degree of blind reasoning not to perceive that in order to find any contradiction here, one would first have to prove that Jesus ever had said that his disciples without faith and spiritual fellowship in and through him could still do the will of the Father and love God and neighbor as they ought, or else show that Jesus had said that it is not through faith and any loving communion with him that we come to love God and neighbor and to do the will of the Father. As far as I know, there has been no attempt to prove either one. Where, then, is the contradiction? Is it not perfectly in order to accede that even as the righteous do not stand in need of repentance, so likewise those who love God and neighbor as they ought to do have no need of a savior? Hence, the question simply is, whether there are any such people to be found in the world? This, however, Jesus denies. Similarly, is it not reasonable to conclude that if only those who believe in Jesus obtain salvation, the unbelievers do not, regardless of how often they cry out, "Lord, Lord! Master! Unparagoned Example!"? Can we reasonably conclude that because Jesus says that it is not possible to obtain salvation merely by addressing him as Lord that, therefore, it is possible, on the basis of his own words, to obtain salvation without acknowledging him as Lord despite the fact that he says, "You call me teacher and Lord; and you are right, for so I am" (John 13:13)? Finally, is it not perfectly in order to conclude that those who by faith become one with the Son are, therefore, obliged to do the will of the Father because the Father and the Son are one? Yes, Jesus says, "This is the work of God, that you believe in him whom he has sent" (John 6:29). "For this is the will of my Father, that every one who sees the Son and believes in him shall have eternal life" (John 6:40).

And yet, does not Jesus categorically declare that he as the Son of man, who executes judgment, will on the last day call those to eternal life who have fed the hungry, clothed the naked, comforted the sick, and exercised love in all matters, thus condemning only those to eternal fire who have failed to show mercy?

Here, there is clearly no mention at all about faith (cf. Matt. 25:31–36; John 5:26–27).

Indeed, this is the conclusion usually drawn wherewith the Lord's enemies triumphantly seek to turn his clear teaching about the faith into a lie. Yet, how far they have been from succeeding in this effort is clearly seen the minute one takes the time needed for a careful reading of the description of the last judgment on which the enemies build their case. First, Jesus describes himself as the all-knowing judge of the world who shall come in glory, accompanied by a multitude of angels, and he presupposes that those whom he acquits perforce acknowledge his divine authority to set them free. Next, it is the sheep that he will set free, that is, those who have heard his voice and followed him as the Good Shepherd who lays down his life for the sheep (cf. John 10:1–18). Finally, he extols their blessedness solely because they fed, clothed, visited, and comforted him through what they did for his brothers, and here it is obvious, of course, that before considering any person as being one with Jesus, one must believe in his divine union or fellowship with those who believe in him. Thus, it follows implicitly, that on that day when all will acknowledge him as Lord, those whom he shall judge praiseworthy cannot possibly call him so with a willing heart without believing that he is the Lord to the glory of God, the Father. Succinctly stated, the thrust of the whole message is that Jesus here lays it upon the hearts of his followers, that it is incumbent upon them that they love him in return for his great love which caused him to give his life for them; and they must be active in love, so that they, for his sake, love those whom he has redeemed. Their love must be expressed in more than empty words; it must manifest itself in action and truth. Yes, who has ever doubted that Jesus was in earnest when he, on the night when he was betrayed, spoke with heavenly feeling to his disciples about love—their love for him and for one another—as the source of genuine joy and truth (cf. John 13:1, 34–35; 14:15–24; 15:9–17, 26)!

If, therefore, we wish to entrap Jesus in his words about love, we shall have to prove, first, that Jesus actually has said that we are able to love him and our neighbor, even as he loves us, and, second, that we can love, for his sake, both without believing in him as well as without receiving his spirit as a gift of grace. Unless we can prove this, we are obliged to admit that Jesus' words about love do not in the slightest degree contradict or weaken his words about faith, but, on the contrary, they do teach us that the saving faith, which Jesus speaks about, is neither a cold nor a lifeless rational assent. Rather, he is speaking of a warm and hearty commitment to all that which, in the providence of God, leads to our blessedness and creates that loving fellowship with God which, conceived in its perfection, is the only true blessedness, even as God is blessed. The true reality of this one and only obtainable blessedness is rooted in the kind of life which is acceptable to God. Outside lie only death and judgment!

In our forefathers' Christianity, the order of salvation was of chief importance. Their salvation was through the faith emanating from Jesus, God's Son and our Savior, and the faith yielded, in turn, love toward him — all in accordance to the unimpeachable authority of his own words. If they, nonetheless, did deviate from his word, it must have been their teaching about the method whereby we can be received and obtain salvation, according to this order: How do we attain the faith and love and, therein, be sustained and grow to eternal and perfect joy?

It is an amply attested fact that our forefathers praised the Word and the Spirit of God, prayer, and the sacraments as the only means whereby we might come to believe in Jesus and grow in his grace and knowledge and, thus, obtain salvation. Consequently, the question is whether or not their thoughts concerning God's stewardship of the kingdom of grace find any authoritative support in Jesus' own words?

Concerning the Holy Spirit, there can hardly be any doubt, in the light of what has preceded, but that Jesus was in agreement with them. Yet, we ought to remember that he testified saying,

"Unless one is born of water and the Spirit, he cannot enter the kingdom of God. That which is born of the flesh is flesh, and that which is born of the Spirit is spirit" (John 3:5–6). "It is the spirit that gives life" (John 6:63). "God is spirit, and those who worship him must worship in spirit and truth" (John 4:24). The spirit which he spoke about was neither an incorporeal part of our nature as human beings nor something attributable to ourselves, but the Spirit of God whom Jesus will send to his disciples from the Father, and whom the Father will send in Jesus' name (cf. John 16:7; 14:16). When Jesus spoke about the truth, he did not allude to a philosophical concept, but pointed to himself as the only begotten who interpreted God to men. Although we have heard this before, we admittedly repeat it here because the customary discussion about spirit and truth is so un-Christian indeed that we might well need to have Jesus' understanding of these words called to mind a second time.

Similarly, Jesus was equally in agreement with our forefathers in regard to the Word of God. Jesus did not only wish that his words would be understood in the strictest sense as God's own words, but he asserted, moreover, that these words of God constituted the means whereby not only the knowledge of God's plan but also God's life-giving Spirit were communicated to those who in faith received the Word. He specifically says,

> He who rejects me and does not receive my sayings has a judge; the word that I have spoken will be his judge on the last day. For I have not spoken on my own authority; the Father who sent me has himself given me commandment what to say and what to speak. And I know that his commandment is eternal life. What I say, therefore, I say as the Father has bidden me. (John 12:48–50)
>
> Do you not believe that I am in the Father and the Father in me? The words that I say to you I do not speak on my own authority. (John 14:10–11a)
>
> I have manifested thy name to the men whom thou gavest me out of the world; thine they were, and thou gavest them to me, and they have kept thy word. . . . I have given them the words which thou gavest me, and they have received them and know in truth

that I came from thee; and they have believed that thou didst send me . . . all mine are thine, and thine are mine. (John 17:6–10)

The words that I have spoken to you are spirit and life. (John 6:63b)

Truly, truly, I say to you, the hour is coming and now is, when the dead will hear the voice of the Son of God, and those who hear will live. (John 5:25)

In their thoughts concerning prayer, our forefathers were not able to reach beyond the thoughts which Jesus expressed when he said,

Watch and pray that you may not enter into temptation. (Matt. 26:41)

Ask, and it will be given you. (Matt. 7:7)

Again I say unto you, if two of you agree on earth about anything they ask, it will be done for them by my Father in heaven. For where two or three are gathered in my name, there I am in the midst of them. (Matt. 18:19–20)

Truly, truly, I say to you, if you ask anything of the Father, he will give it to you in my name . . . ask, and you will receive, that your joy may be made full. (John 16:23–24)

Whatever you ask in my name, I will do it, that the Father may be glorified in the Son; if you ask anything in my name, I will do it. (John 14:13)

Regarding their thoughts concerning the Spirit, the Word, and prayer in the name of Jesus, the forefathers were, according to Jesus' own words, completely in the right. Consequently, the only remaining question is that of the sacraments, or strictly construed, the so-called means of grace, for it cannot be denied that there appears to be a great difference between these means of grace and those already mentioned. Admittedly, the Word is something physical; yet simultaneously it is also something spiritual, because it is the Spirit's natural vehicle for expression. On the contrary, the baptismal water and the wine and bread in the Lord's Supper are purely physical, tangible things which therefore would appear to be far less suitable vehicles for the Spirit.

Nevertheless, Jesus said, "Go therefore and make disciples of all nations, baptizing them in the name of the Father and of the Son and of the Holy Spirit" (Matt. 28:19). "Truly, truly, I say to you, unless one is born anew, he cannot see the kingdom of God. . . . Unless one is born of water and the Spirit, he cannot enter the kingdom of God" (John 3:3, 5). Thus, it is evident that Jesus spoke of the water in baptism as an inseparable part of the spiritual regeneration without which one cannot anew become a child of God. Hence he gave the forefathers the right to declare baptism essential for salvation. However, it is doubtful whether this gave them the right to condemn those whose baptism they had not witnessed.

Similarly, speaking about the bread in the Lord's Supper, Jesus said, "Take, eat; this is my body," and about the wine he said, "Drink of it all of you, for this is my blood of the covenant, which is poured out for many for the forgiveness of sins" (Matt. 26:26–28). Those who in faith took him at his word, that we are to eat his flesh and drink his blood in order to be saved, could not possibly think otherwise but that this mysterious fellowship with him in the Spirit is granted particularly through the bread and the wine (cf. John 6:52–59). Thus the one and only point of uncertainty that could arise would be whether all Christians would be under obligation to take part in the Lord's Supper — never any uncertainty as to whether the communicants were bound to believe that they thereby entered into the most intimate and complete union with him, the crucified and risen Lord.

Since the forefathers together with Luther never maintained that the Lord's Supper is essential for salvation, but adhered strictly to the words "He who believes and is baptized will be saved . . ." (Mark 16:16), it cannot be said that on this point they disregarded Jesus' own words. Hence if they have done this with any of the doctrines in the Augsburg Confession, it must have been concerning the doctrines of original sin (Article 2) and free will (Article 18). Inasmuch as this teaching does not contradict any of Jesus' words, we have ever more reason for boldly declaring that which we have heard, namely, that Jesus addresses all human beings as sinners, standing in need of being set free by the Son. He explicitly testifies, "Truly, truly, I say to you, every one who commits sin is a slave of sin. . . . So if the Son makes you free, you will be free indeed" (John 8:34, 36). Therefore, Christian theology must always proceed, even with regard to Jesus' own words, from the presupposition that every human being came into this present life born in sin and spiritual bondage, and thus totally unable to be liberated, acquitted, and well pleasing to God apart from faith in the Son, Jesus Christ. We limit our confession to this very statement with no desire to employ scholastic sophistry in order to either determine the manner in which sinfulness is reproduced or specify the conditions of the will apart from the moral relationship to God and to true, that is, spiritual, righteousness.

However, let us assume for the moment that this presupposition may be just as questionable as when an individual hazards, as frequently happens, to infer that he knows the thoughts of another person, even though that individual has not explicitly said so. Thus, this does not in the slightest degree disprove the genuineness of the forefathers' Christianity. For it is equally true that regardless of how we may prefer to express ourselves concerning original sin and free will, we are called upon, according to Jesus' words, to believe that we stand in need of the forgiveness of sin and deliverance from the bondage of sin by faith in him. Obviously, this was the only point which the forefathers wanted to emphasize in their confessional statements concerning original sin and free will.

Furthermore, it must be indicated that despite the fact that we cannot point to words of Jesus which precisely express all the doctrinal statements in our forefathers' confession, there might, nevertheless, very well have been statements attributable to him which directed those who believed in him to another source of knowledge from which they deduced these particular tenets.

Even so, they built as exclusively upon his words as if he had stated what he demands of us with respect to the way in which we listen to others. For the observant reader of the Gospels there is not the slightest doubt as to whether Jesus actually has referred us, in part, to the sacred writings of Moses, David, and the prophets, and, partly, to his apostles. The former were his trustworthy heralds who announced his coming and spoke of its cause and consequences, and the latter were the true spokesmen and duly recognized interpreters of his teachings. Consequently, whatever may be claimed legitimately with respect to the prophets and the apostles rests, moreover, on Jesus' own words.

Concerning the sacred writings of the Jewish people, Jesus declares:

Scripture cannot be broken. (John 10:35)

You search the scriptures, because you think that in them you have eternal life; and it is they that bear witness to me. (John 5:39)

Think not that I have come to abolish the law and the prophets; I have come not to abolish them but to fulfill them. For truly, I say to you, till heaven and earth pass away, not an iota, not a dot, will pass from the law until all is accomplished. (Matt. 5:17-18)

If they do not hear Moses and the prophets, neither will they be convinced if some one should rise from the dead. (Luke 16:31)

Speaking from a Christian perspective, there is really nothing adverse to say about the Old Testament's proofs; yet, even so, we do not stand in need of them, for on the basis of Jesus' words to and about his apostles, we should not regard them as something requisite. Speaking to the apostles, Jesus says,

Go therefore and make disciples of all nations, baptizing them in the name of the Father and of the Son and of the Holy Spirit, teaching them to observe all that I have commanded you; and, lo, I am with you always, to the close of the age. (Matt. 28:19-20) But the Counselor, the Holy Spirit, whom the Father will send in my name, He will teach you all things, and bring to your remembrance all that I have said to you. (John 14:26) I have yet many things to say to you, but you cannot bear them now. When the Spirit of truth comes, He will guide you into all the truth; . . . He will glorify me. (John 16:12–14) Truly, truly, I say to you, he who receives any one whom I send receives me; and he who receives me receives him who sent me. (John 13:20) As the Father has sent me, even so I send you. (John 20:21) And if any one will not receive you or listen to your words, shake off the dust from your feet as you leave that house or town. Truly, I say to you, it shall be more tolerable on that day of judgment for the land of Sodom and Gomorrah than for that town. (Matt. 10:14–15) For it is not you who speak, but the Spirit of your Father speaking through you. (Matt. 10:20)

On the basis of these sayings, it is evident that Jesus intended that after his departure all should come to believe in him by and through the preaching of the apostles. Similarly, prior to his going away, Jesus prayed especially for the apostles and for those who would come to believe in him as a result of their message; he prayed that they might be one in him and in the Father (cf. John 17). Therefore, it is not a subject of inquiry as to whether we are obliged to accept the apostles' explanations as Jesus' own, and receive them as his words, passed on to us, without further explanation, in fully intelligible statements concerning his teachings.

Against this point of view, the rationalistic theologians protest with all their might by insisting that the apostles did not understand Jesus' message; but they, on the contrary, do understand his words, and thereby conclude that the Christianity which the apostles propagated was entirely unauthenticated, presumably a flash of wit and merriment on their part. It is to the apostles that Jesus, while speaking about the coming of the Holy Spirit, solemnly declares that they are the best and only rightful interpreters of his words. However, as far as I know, the rationalists have not made any whispering statement of having received any formal testimony from him, much less of having received a mandate authorizing them to examine the apostles. Who can, even for a moment, have faith in Jesus without believing that he himself knew better than the eighteenth-century theologians what he thought and how he intended to have his words explained? As to who is really the wisest with respect to spiritual, heavenly, and divine things is a question which we, for the time being, shall allow to stand on its own merits. Who are really the wisest? Yesterday's theologians, who readily admit that they do not know whence they came and where they are going and know even less about the secrets of God, or he who testified, "I came from the Father and have come into the world; again, I am leaving the world and going to the Father" (John 16:28); "I say to you, we speak of what we know, and bear witness of what we have seen" (John 3:11). Yes, we plead with these learned gentlemen that they by all means allow us to direct our inquiry concerning what Christ taught as well as what he said to those who had heard him and had been appointed by him to teach all mankind about the only true, authentic Christianity. If, after having been adequately informed, we were to discover that Christianity is unworthy of belief, we simply should have to bite into the sour apple and thus relieve ourselves of the truly disheartening experience of being disciples of masters of theology who personally confess that they, in reality, do not know what is eternally true about spiritual things. Apparently, the sole exception here is the always underlying rationale that they—whose reason knows nothing—nevertheless claim to know everything concerning what is worthy of knowledge. However, they must not proffer their wisdom to us under the guise of Christianity. If we should have found the true authentic Christianity to be unacceptable, why would we opt for that which is false and consequently far inferior as it fails to measure up to the name which has been stolen from the true Christianity? This is surely despicable if Christianity is true, and terribly stupid if Christianity is but a lie. However, we cannot deny the unprecedented situation that many of the enemies and despisers of Christianity have found it advantageous to assume its name. Yes, this very circumstance arouses in us the strong supposition that the genuine, apostolic Christianity must be essentially good and clearly have demonstrated this quality. Surely, that man must have infinitely much to offer or at least be beyond reproach whose enemies assume his name in order to win by cunning what cannot be gained by sheer power.

3

Trustworthy and Authoritative Witnesses

Whenever any person demands that the validity of all Christian articles of faith must be proven by Jesus' own words, we face a question which, indeed, may lead to two antithetical views: either we understand, thereby, that the Gospels in their testimony concerning the words and deeds of Jesus do not necessarily contain everything that all Christians must believe—and in this sense I appropriate the words as my own—or we take the question under consideration to mean that Christians are not demanded to believe anything unless Jesus Christ wills to descend visibly in order to communicate the Word to us. Obviously, this is the point of view of those who argue against the apostles' authority in matters of faith. If the apostles' witness concerning the person of Jesus, his words, and deeds are not trustworthy, we simply do not know anything about them. Also, if the apostles' witness to these things is not infallible, we can no more draw a conclusion on the basis of the words of Jesus passed on to us by the apostles than we can be certain that it was exactly these words, and in this context, which Jesus would have wanted to constitute the rule of faith for his church. Nonetheless, it is nowadays the theologians' unfortunate habit, on the one hand, to elevate Jesus' words to the one and only divine rule of faith, and, on the other hand, to assert that we do not have one single word of Jesus upon which we can build with full certainty. It most clearly and necessarily follows that for us as Christians there is absolutely nothing to believe except the surely absurd statement that if Jesus Christ were to speak to us, which he of course does not, then we should finally come to believe in him and rest our hope of salvation solely on his word. I call this a foolish sentence because either the apostles' testimony concerning Jesus is trustworthy or it is not; but if it is trustworthy, we must believe it. If the testimony is not reliable, we simply do not have the slightest assurance that Jesus actually lived, and much less that he was a man in whom we could and should believe in matters concerning spiritual things and God's hidden way of salvation for sinners! On the contrary, we are rationally bound to conclude that if he, who desired to have all people believe that the words he uttered were, indeed, words of God and of eternal life, had not provided for making his pure and infallible words known to his believers, he either has never lived on the earth or he must have been deranged. In that case he is no more to be trusted than the poor, unlearned fishermen, tax collectors, and tentmakers who took upon themselves the foolish task of teaching other people what they themselves did not know anything about: namely, God's way of eternal salvation. It is quite apparent that if Jesus were not the Son of God, essentially one with the Father, it would be idolatry to believe in him and to worship him. If he did not know God in the same way that God knew him, then his testimony concerning God's secret counsel would be completely untenable. However, if he were the only begotten Son, who spoke what he had heard from the Father, and had been given "all authority in heaven and on earth" (Matt. 28:18), he naturally would take steps to firmly establish his words on the earth. Indeed, this was a matter of urgency for his words constituted the one, great gospel: the message of God's grace and the words of eternal life to all generations! However, Jesus Christ is not visibly present on earth today. Moreover, he has left us no books written by himself. Wherefore, either his words must have been passed on without distortion and rightly interpreted by those who heard him or we simply know neither what he said nor what he thought. If the latter actually should be the case, we would not have the slightest interest in the grossly pretentious claim attributed to him, that his words would endure, even when heaven and earth would cease to exist (cf. Luke 21:33). On the contrary, we should be compelled to let such words be silenced and regarded as rumors circulated by the common people right after the rulers took the liberty to crucify him in the hope of silencing his voice for ever, even as they had done to others! There is no clear way in which we can escape making a choice: either we receive his commissioned messengers, that is, the apostles, as his true representatives and accept their words, spoken in his name, as his own — all in accordance with what we are commanded to do in the name of Jesus Christ — or we are, in truth, what the pagans always have called us: "fools for Christ's sake" (1 Cor. 9–10). In such a case, we should have no advantage over Turks and pagans except for the ridiculous notion that a certain unknown teaching, traceable to an otherwise unknown person by the name of Jesus Christ, made us children of God and heirs of heaven. Indeed, to people of rational nature this teaching was a superstition which they would be ashamed to consider. By their own refutation, they made the Christians proverbial among the Jews, Turks, and pagans. For to appeal to the words of a man, which some admittedly regard as most uncertain, in order to base one's advantage and build one's hope of salvation upon a teaching which oneself declares to be an obscure tale, the real meaning of which some highly learned scholar may or may not be able to conjecture, is, in truth, foolish. It is as mindless and ridiculous as the most rageful enemies of Christianity could wish!

Thus, if we now have perceived that everything which is said about Christianity is wasted and clearly nonsensical unless the apostles are regarded as trustworthy witnesses and reliable interpreters of the sayings of Jesus, we have drawn, thereby, a sharp line of demarcation between the Christian and the non-Christian theologians. For the theologian who calls in question the authority of the apostles is equally as un-Christian as the one who entertains doubts about the historical validity of the New Testament. Yes, he must surely know that if the apostles have not spoken clearly and unequivocally with regard to what constitutes authentic and undistorted Christianity, neither he nor all the theologians in the world would be able to inform us. Any one who would take upon himself the task of communicating to others what he himself cannot possibly know would simply either make a fool of his audience or make himself appear to be a fool! Consequently, any theologian who believes that the apostles' memories have failed them when they quote Jesus' sayings, or what amounts to the same, believes that they have misunderstood and misinterpreted his words, must perforce—if he is an honest and intelligent man—declare without any reservation that, according to his conviction, there neither is nor can be any basic Christian theology but only a historical-philological dispute about this peculiar book which the Christians call the *New Testament.* Similarly, he must boldly maintain that if the apostles actually have written what is ascribed to them they must have been not only ignorant and credulous persons, but uncouth idolaters, and egotistical and maniacal enthusiasts. It is very manifest that they attributed divine honor to their Master and desired expressly to have their witness about his sayings, as well as their interpretation of his words, accepted and believed as an ever unfailing word of God. According to Matthew's formal assurance, Jesus declared that what the apostles were to proclaim in his name would not be their own utterances but the Spirit of God speaking through them (cf. Matt. 10:26). And according to John's formal assurance, Jesus said that the Spirit of truth, the Father's own Holy Spirit, would both assist their remembrance and guide them "into all the truth" (John 14:26; 16:13), thus teaching them all things: things to come and things past. Even if there were those who contended that Jesus had not spoken in this way, the apostles, nevertheless, believed, and moreover deliberately sought to have all Chris-

60

tians believe what Jesus had said concerning these things. In-deed, whoever propagates such ideas about divine knowledge and infallibility must either be absolutely certain about his mission, and his call and authority or he must find satisfaction in being looked upon as a pitiful mixture of a maniacal en-thusiast and a deliberate deceiver!

In other words, only apostolic Christianity is really authentic. Yet in our frantic times, many of us have heard theologians say to us that they, as well-enlightened Christians, do not share the apostles' faith, but only Jesus Christ's own faith, and therefore do not believe in the Son but only in the Father. This is patently absurd, not only because one thereby makes one's own being and relation to God wholly equal to that of God's only begotten Son, but because it is self-evident that these very theologians are precisely in the same position as we: namely, neither they nor we can know anything about the faith of Jesus Christ apart from what the apostles narrate. Thus, according to their sure tes-timony, Jesus told them that they all should believe and honor the Son, just as they honored the Father, and never imagine that they could come to the Father except by the Son, who in every respect is both the way and the door, and the truth and the life (cf. John 5:23; 10:1–9; 14:6)!

If now the apostles have imparted to us, through written form, the oral teachings of Jesus without any explanation, we must assume that their account of what he said is sufficiently intelli-gible and therefore simply build thereon with confidence. But if they either originally incorporated or later added an explana-tion, then we must take Jesus' words in that particular sense which they as appointed and authorized interpreters regard as the correct meaning. Thus, we see here that when our fore-fathers credited the apostles' words with the same validity as Jesus' own words, they simply did what was and still is neces-sary in order to come to know Jesus' own words as well as to continue to abide by them! If seen from a certain perspective, they might have infringed, even the least, upon the glory and power of Jesus. This could have happened by erroneously crediting words which were not of apostolic origin as words of the apostles. This could happen again either by crediting false words as apostolic or overlooking the difference which the apostles themselves drew between their valid, apostolic explanations and their private, Christian opinions only.

As we now, following this introduction which in our day is highly necessary, even though some perhaps may deem it superfluous, turn our attention to the apostles' special use and interpretation of the words of Jesus, we are certain to discover that our forefathers and Luther both together depended upon wholly reliable sources for all of their doctrines which definitely are rooted in that apostolic teaching that constitutes the Christians' one and only unalterable rule of faith. It will not do to object by saying that it is possible to find statements and assertions in the works of the Lutheran theologians and, perhaps, even in Luther's own writings, which are not quite in accord with the apostles' teachings, or apparently not even found therein, because Luther and the theologians of his school could not have been Christians if they had ascribed to themselves the infallibility and authority over the church's faith which they on biblical grounds denied the pope. Surely, no one questions what history most clearly shows, namely, that Luther and his helpers presented their confession of faith to the church as a statement of confessional unity which all evangelical Christians should agree upon; and that their theology should be evaluated according to the rule of faith; and, last, that especially Martin Luther most solemnly took the position that he would repudiate any of his opinions which possibly could be found contradicting God's Word in the Holy Bible.

Hence, we shall allow the Lutheran theology to stand upon its own merits, even as Martin Luther allowed the theology of the church fathers to stand or fall solely upon the ultimate criterion: the Word. We hold to the Lutheran, that is, the Augsburg Confession, and have no difficulty in finding well-grounded evidence in the writings of the apostles, even for those statements which could be questioned, especially if the Gospels contained only the words of Jesus.

Here, too, we shall begin with what we know about the person of Jesus Christ, his mission, and his church, because we are all cognizant of the fact that, according to the forefathers' firm opinion and also according to the very nature of the inquiry itself, the foremost question among Christians centers upon Christ's person, mission, and church. What must we believe about him in order to be true disciples of Jesus Christ? Dare we, as true disciples, look forward to him in hope? And, finally, what characterizes, at the very present time, the relationship between the true disciples and Jesus Christ?

Yes, Jesus of Nazareth—who was crucified under Pontius Pilate, died, and was buried, and on the third day rose again—is the Christ. He is the Messiah, the Lord's anointed, the king of Israel, whose sovereign power defies the times (cf. John 1:41). He is the high priest "for ever after the order of Melchizedek" who offered his own life as a sacrifice for sin (cf. Hebrews 7; Psalm 110). He is the Savior from sin, death, and judgment whose coming was predicted by the prophets of Israel and awaited by posterity (cf. John 4:25–26). Here we have the apostles' undeniable teaching, supported by Jesus' own words about the purpose of his coming. In addition to these words which they have passed on to us, we have the apostles' repeated assurance that what happened to Jesus of Nazareth was bound to take place according to the prophets' predictions about the promised one of the seed of Abraham and of the house of David, through whom "all the families of the earth will be blessed" (Acts 3:25; Gal. 3:8). Relative hereto, it generally suffices to refer to the Gospel according to Matthew, where we find from the beginning to the end, from the conception to the death of Jesus, the same testimony recurring. However, if further assurance is needed, it is readily found in the Gospel according to John, the Acts of the Apostles, and the Epistles. For this reason, our forefathers were not only within their full right in assuming that both of the Testaments, the Old and the New, constitute, in effect, a unity centered in Christ, but they were also cognizant of being under the necessity of sharing a common faith and teaching with the apostles (cf. Heb. 1:1–2). Indeed, this ought to be the wish of all true Christians, for it cannot be denied that the apostles are the first Christians and also Christianity's especially appointed representatives in the world. Even so, there may well be a difference of opinion among Christians with respect to the Old Testament; opinions which the apostles neither have stated explicitly nor sought to explain, because they are not witnessing to a book containing a given number of pages, but about the message of the prophets. Their own testimony concerning the utterances of the prophets is that they require interpretation in order to be rightly understood, and that Jesus Christ and the Holy Spirit alone are able to give the proper interpretation. Therefore, it is altogether impossible to reprove the Lutheran theologians when they contend that, according to the very nature of Christianity, it is incumbent upon us to regard the prophets of Israel as instruments of God's Spirit, and, in the name of the Lord, accept their words as God's, and, finally, accept the apostolic interpretation of Israel's prophets as divinely inspired (cf. Acts 7:38). However, they are fully responsible for any of their decisions regarding the extent of the canon of Holy Scripture and the proper use of the Scriptures, unless they can present clear evidence in the writings of the apostles in support of their decisions. It is, of course, within the right of scholars and schools to seek to corroborate the relation between the New and Old Testaments in order to prove their proposition that the Old Testament confirms the validity of the New. But in the church, the Old Testament is confirmed by, or borrows its validity, from the New. Therefore, every question to which there is no clear answer in the New Testament must simply be regarded as unsettled, without having any school or theologians of any period impose their theories concerning the same upon the church, as if these theories were Christian articles of faith. Otherwise, the theologians will be acting contrary to the New Testament's precept by making themselves masters of the church's faith instead of being always the servants of the church (cf. 2 Cor. 4:5). Yes, nowadays the majority of theologians have been tempted and obsessed by this domineering spirit from which all papal and hierarchal powers spring. What is hierarchy except domination by the clergy, and what is papal power but self-made Christianity to be forced upon the church of Christ! Unfortunately, people are on the whole too undiscerning to recognize either papal power or clerical rule, except in those situations in which they appear in their most distasteful form. Without equivocation, it is certainly clear that the moment the opinions of the theologians are to be equated with Christianity, the church is held in spiritual captivity. On the next day, the captors need only demand that because of their spiritual gifts, they deserve to receive the church's emoluments and thus gain social status among all who regard them as Christ's representatives on earth and the apostles' successors who alone have the key to the Scripture and the right to make out of it whatever they desire! God, grant that the eyes of the church members may be opened to see the threatening danger before it is too late. Yes, that they may see how the rationalistic theologians by their continuous outburst of criticism against hierarchy and papacy lead, often unknown to themselves, all their blindfolded followers right into the same onerous kind of papalism. As the Lord says, "If a blind man leads a blind man, both will fall into a pit" (Matt. 15:14).

We shall leave it to history to determine to what extent this theological imperiousness can be detected among our highly learned forefathers. Indeed, this imperiousness is far remote from the Augsburg Confession, as all of its Christian readers know and ought to declare openly. We find no teachings in the Augsburg Confession which are not sufficiently rooted in the writings of the apostles. This is my firm conviction, which I believe I already have defended by the passages which I have cited. Nevertheless, for further support, I shall at this point bring into view additional passages from the writings of the apostles. It is well known that the apostle John ends his testimony about Jesus Christ by saying, "Now Jesus did many other signs in the presence of the disciples, which are not written in this book; but these are written that you may believe that Jesus is the Christ, the Son of God, and that believing you may have life in his name" (John 20:30, 31). This clearly indicates that John desired to have all of Jesus' self-testimonies concerning his divinity and indispensability for salvation accepted and believed verbatim, words which John has passed on to us. With full assurance, the apostle John opens his gospel by testifying that Jesus Christ, who lived his genuine, human life on earth and showed us his glory, is the living and creative Word of God—consubstantial with the Father—through whom "all things were made" and from whom that light shines forth which "enlightens every man" (John 1:9). Yes, "to all who received him, who believed in his name, he gave power to become the children of God" (John 1:12). In recent times, theologians have argued vehemently about what John meant by the term: the Word. He employs the term to signify the true divinity of the person of Jesus. The theologians, however, have even expressed the thought that if the word "reason" is the best translation of the Greek word *logos,* then, in effect, the testimony concerning Jesus' divinity falls to the ground. Indeed, such a view reflects immature thinking. Regardless of whether we translate *logos* into "word" or "reason" or some other equivalent word, John clearly testifies that Jesus is the divine *logos* by whom all things are created, and from whom all light and life emanate, and that only by faith in his name are we able to obtain a heavenly childlikeness and the right "to become children of God" (John 1:12). This is the point of the matter, and not whether it is preferable, in speaking Danish, to call God's only begotten Son "his Word" or "his reason," which, logically speaking, may well be a legitimate, grammatical, and philosophical question. However, it is never a question at issue for the church because the answer to the inquiry cannot change, even in the smallest degree, John's testimony concerning the divinity of Jesus Christ and eternal salvation through faith in his name (cf. John 1:12; 1 John 5:13).

Right from the beginning to the end, the apostle John has made every effort to be sure that there would be no doubt in the minds of the readers of his Gospel regarding what he himself believed and endeavored to have others believe about his Lord and Master, whom he loved. Moreover, he has added a brief explanation to specific sayings of the Lord which are altogether too unique to be passed over. Accordingly, where Jesus is quoted saying, "Now is the judgment of this world, now shall the ruler of this world be cast out, and I, when I am lifted up from the earth, will draw all men to myself" (John 12:31–32), John adds, "He said this to show by what death he was to die" (John 12:32). Indeed, this explanation was necessary in order for us to relate the "lifting up" from the earth to the crucifixion, and be assured, moreover, that this was Jesus' intended meaning. Otherwise it might seem fully as reasonable to conclude that Jesus thereby pointed to his ascension. The explanation is significant not only with respect to these words of Jesus, but also to such words as when he says, "As Moses lifted up the serpent in the wilderness, so must the Son of man be lifted up, that whoever believes in him may have eternal life" (John 3:14, 15). As we here consider the imagery of the brazen serpent to which Jesus makes reference, we cannot but think of his crucifixion. Even though Jesus has spoken about his ascension in the preceding sentence, we should have grave misgivings in the church about insisting upon applying this "lifting up"—in order that those who had been bitten by the serpents might be saved from death—to the crucifixion, except for the fact that the apostle explicitly has testified that Jesus' purpose in being "lifted up" from the earth was none other than to save us from the ruler of this world and transfer us to the kingdom of God's beloved Son! Now, by comparison, we clearly see that the death of Jesus upon the cross must, indeed, as our forefathers and Luther believed and taught, be recognized by all Christians as the event to which the salvation of sinners and their eternal life are inseparably linked. That this was a matter close to the heart of the apostle is, perhaps, best revealed by his comment on Caiaphas's advice to the religious leaders. Caiaphas said, "It is expedient for the people that one man should die for the people, and not that the whole nation should perish" (John 11:50). John comments by saying, "He did not say this of his own accord, but being high priest that year he prophesied that Jesus should die for the nation, and not for the nation only, but to gather into one the children of God who are scattered abroad" (John 11:51–52). Here it is well to note that the thoughts expressed on this topic in his apostolic letter are equally clear to the observant reader. Thus, when he witnesses that "the blood of Jesus his Son cleanses us from all sin" (1 John 1:7) and that "he is the expiation for our sins, and not for ours only but also for the sins of the whole world" (1 John 2:2), we immediately perceive that, according to the apostle's testimony, it was by his self-sacrificing death that Jesus took away our sins, and bestowed, through the power of his name, the forgiveness of sins to those who believed in his name (cf. 1 John 3:23; 5:13). If this be the case, there can be no doubt but that the atonement, accomplished by the death of Jesus upon the cross, was the Son's supreme, earthly mission. Wherefore the apostle also says, "The reason the Son of God appeared was to destroy the works of the devil" (1 John 3:8). Moreover, we know, according to the words of Jesus and his apostle, that this was only brought to pass by the death of Jesus on the cross.

There is no question but that Jesus' unequivocal words, which the apostle has passed on to us without any annotation, brought about the apostle's conviction that the Son essentially is one with the Father, and that the believers likewise are, in truth, one with the Son (cf. John 17:21; 1 John 1:3). Thus, at the very beginning of his Gospel, John emphatically declares that Jesus Christ together with the Father is God and the source of life (cf.

John 1:1–4). However, the apostle also clearly testifies, "No one who denies the Son has the Father. He who confesses the Son has the Father also" (1 John 2:23). "And this is the testimony that God gave us eternal life, and this life is in his Son. He who has the Son has life; he who has not the Son has not life" (1 John 5:11, 12).

Concerning the Holy Spirit, some apparently have been of the opinion that if it were possible to disregard the mode of expressing the view that there are three who testify in heaven—the Father, the Word, and the Holy Spirit—and that these three are one, then they would be unfettered by John's testimony about the Holy Spirit as a divine, personal Being. Thus, they would be free to take what he says in his Epistle concerning the Spirit of God and Jesus as a discourse on the Christian heart and mind born out of imagination or reason. Here, however, they are curiously in error. First of all, we must also remember that it is none other than the apostle John who here has communicated to us Jesus' explicit words about the Holy Spirit's distinct relation to the Deity. He has transmitted these words to us without the slightest hint that they were to be understood differently than when originally heard. This is, in itself, sufficient testimony. Therefore, where the apostle speaks about the Spirit of God, we must, consequently, presuppose that very personal Spirit of truth whom he himself in his Gospel has taught us through the words of Jesus to recognize, to hope for, and by which to be comforted. Thus, when John testifies, among other things, that Jesus "breathed on them and said to them, 'Receive the Holy Spirit'" (John 20:22), not even an assurance by John could make us believe that these words of Jesus simply were to be understood in terms of a rationalistic mode of Christian thought. Indeed, for any person to allege such stupidity of John, who has given no occasion whatsoever for such an assertion, would be most irresponsible. Yet, when the apostle quotes Jesus as saying, "He who believes in me, as the Scripture has said, 'Out of his heart shall flow rivers of living water'" (John 7:38), he adds a brief note in which he, on his part, disavows any possible participation whatsoever in expounding the self-made concept of the Holy Spirit which was prevalent among the rationalists of his day. He testifies, "Now this he said about the Spirit, which those who believed in him were to receive; for as yet the Spirit had not been given because Jesus was not yet glorified" (John 7:39). As to how these words are to be understood is not an issue at this point where the question simply is: What did the apostles think concerning the Holy Spirit? Seen in this perspective, the words are indisputably clear. It is quite obvious that the apostle has no intention of depriving himself or his fellow disciples, who believed in the Lord, of a Christian mode of thinking. Hence, when the apostle writes that the believers "abide in him, and he in them. And by this we know that he abides in us, by the Spirit which he has given us" (1 John 3:24), we presumably understand him. However, if we do need to be reminded that he means a personal Spirit, we have a corroboratory statement in which he says, "Beloved, do not believe every spirit, but test the spirits to see whether they are of God . . . every spirit which confesses that Jesus Christ has come in the flesh is of God, and every spirit which does not confess Jesus is not of God. This is the spirit of antichrist . . ." (1 John 4:1). Here, however, we shall take no note of what in our perception either is or at least appears to be obscure, for the way that we intend to use it is manifestly clear, because when the apostle makes the confession of Jesus Christ the criterion by which to test the presence of the Spirit of God, he speaks undeniably about a personal spirit which communicates. Contrarily, it is obvious that the rationalists' so-called Spirit of God and of Christ has absolutely nothing to proclaim. If the truthfulness of the rationalists' so-called spirit cannot even be tested, so as to determine whether it is identical with what the apostle calls the Spirit of God or simply nothing but antichrist's deaf and dumb spirit seeking to avoid any critical testing by neither confessing nor denying Jesus

Christ, then there is no escape from the judgment which the apostle pronounces upon every spirit which does not confess!

Thus, this is the Johannine Christianity which the critics persistently have contrasted with what they regard as the only true Christianity, namely, the Pauline. It probably is much easier to distort John's than Paul's words, because John usually presupposes the faith and emphatically lays stress upon that love without which the faith is dead. Yet, it is as clear as the noonday sun that John, like Peter and Paul, believed that we are sinners and that faith in Jesus Christ as a divine person, who died that we might live with him, is the only way by which we can obtain the forgiveness of our sins, and be empowered to become children of God, and thus share in that eternal life of the Son which God and the Son grant unto us through the Holy Spirit!

Even though the two witnesses, Matthew and John, are sufficient for our purpose, we do wish to hear, nevertheless, what the apostle Peter says about these things. Admittedly, Peter has not left a written gospel for posterity; nonetheless, it might be expected normally that in the writings of an apostle addressed to the Church, we will be able to discern the Christian articles of faith, regardless of whether they are specifically pointed out or merely presupposed.

As we closely peruse the First Letter of Peter, the very first thing that attracts our attention is that the apostle addresses himself to Christians (4:16). He defines Christians as people who believe in Jesus Christ, the crucified, risen, and ascended Lord who "is at the right hand of God, with angels, authorities and powers subject to him" (3:22). The apostle admonishes these Christian people to be steadfast in the faith, and in love follow the example of the Lord whom they confess and on whom they build their hope of eternal salvation. This is sufficient, indeed, to show that the apostle Peter, in the name of Jesus Christ, expounded the same teachings as Matthew and John. Thus, also in this letter we are able to trace all the fundamental

Christian doctrines that we have learned from the words of Jesus and the testimony of the writers of the Gospels. Hence, Peter reminds the Christians that it was "the Spirit of Christ" which revealed to the prophets of Israel God's way of salvation and foretold both the trials and the subsequent glory which the Christians would share with their Lord (1:6–12). Thereby, Peter confesses that he, like Matthew and John, accepts the words of the prophets as God's word, and he attaches the same significance as they do to the suffering of Christ. Indeed, the entire message centers around the physical and eternal glory which Christ will share with the believers, that is, "God's own people" (2:9), who "were ransomed . . . not with . . . silver or gold but with the precious blood of Christ" (1:19) when he suffered for sinners "the righteous for the unrighteous, that he might bring us to God" (3:18). Yes, the apostle emphatically declares that Christ himself "bore our sins in his body on the tree that we might die to sin and live to righteousness. By his wounds you have been healed" (2:24). The apostle Peter does not in any way allow us to cast doubt on what in his view constitutes Christ's chief mission on earth. Thus, there is no question in his mind but that Jesus' self-sacrifice on the cross was the great, heroic deed whereby he saved us. Hence, the faith centered upon his death on the cross effects in us the transfer from the state of death to life. According to Peter, the Holy Spirit is distinguished from the human; it is the personal and communicating spirit of God, the source of the prophets' and apostles' preaching; and it is the power whereby the Christians, to whom he wrote, were sanctified and made steadfast in the faith. For as he says, "If you are reproached for the name of Christ, you are blessed, because the spirit of glory and of God rests upon you" (4:15). On the basis of what he says, it would be most imprudent indeed if we were to interpret his words as expressive of that rationalistic view of the Holy Spirit which is at one with that pagan mode of thought which does not lead us to endure, but results in blasphemies wherever the name of Jesus Christ is confessed.

Indeed, the apostle Peter looked upon himself and all other persons as sinners who only in Jesus' name could be saved from judgment and prepared for the inheritance of the saints in the light with Christ. This is unquestionably implied in what we have heard. Moreover, it is substantiated by what we read in his letter, "For you were straying like sheep, but have returned to the Shepherd and Guardian of your souls" (2:25). He states that prior to their conversion, they did "what the Gentiles like to do, living in licentiousness . . . and lawless idolatry" (4:3). Only the God of all grace, who has called us to his eternal glory in Christ, can nourish, strengthen, confirm, and establish us. Yes, we read, "Blessed be the God and Father of our Lord Jesus Christ! By his great mercy we have been born anew to a living hope . . . and to an inheritance which is imperishable, undefiled, and unfading, kept in heaven for you who by God's power are guarded through faith. . . . As the outcome of your faith you obtain the salvation of your souls" (1:3 – 5, 9).

In closing, it should be noted that Peter emphatically attributes a saving and life-renewing power to Holy Baptism when he witnesses that "Baptism . . . now saves you . . . as an appeal to God for a clear conscience through the resurrection of Jesus Christ" (3:21). Thus, it is quite obvious that Peter definitely is thinking of the Christian baptism by water, for he bids us to regard baptism "not as a removal of dirt from the body" (3:21), but as a spiritual means of grace that may be compared with that salvation which in the days of Noah was effected "through water" (3:20). Nevertheless, there was a difference. In that day only those who were on board the ark, which was borne by the water, were saved. In baptism, on the contrary, we are, figuratively speaking, immersed and drowned in the water. At first sight, this is admittedly an abstruse teaching, but only because of the very condensed form in which he expresses his view. In any case, it cannot be denied that the apostle is speaking about Christian baptism by water and accredits it, as a means in the hand of God, with saving power. This is for us as Christians of vital importance. Moreover, we have the words of Jesus to the effect that all who wish to become his disciples must be baptized (cf. Matt. 28:18–20), and in the Gospel according to John, Jesus emphatically declares, "Unless one is born of water and the Spirit, he cannot see the kingdom of God" (John 3:5). Admittedly, any attempt to understand what this means could easily cause doubt in our minds if we did not have an apostle testifying to the essentiality of baptism for salvation (cf. Acts 2:38–39, 41).

We could conclude the discussion here, for even if we did not make use of Paul's testimony, we nevertheless would not lack testimonies in support of each of the articles of faith contained in the Augsburg Confession and acknowledged by our forefathers. Obviously, if our forefathers failed to build on Paul's testimony, it certainly was not because they, at his behest, embraced any teaching which was not sufficiently rooted in the words of Jesus and his apostles. Rather, if they failed in this matter, perhaps, it might have been because they, without valid reason, placed Paul on a par with the apostles who were called and commissioned by the Lord during his earthly presence among them.

Whenever the subject of Paul's apostolic authority is discussed within the church, the one great question which continuously arises centers around the authenticity of the writings ascribed to the apostles of Jesus Christ. Do we have any assurance that these writings really are authentic? Thus, not until the apostolicity of a given writing has been proven are we ready to consider whether other writings should be accorded the same distinction. The church can neither be unaware of, nor should it conceal, the present-day recurrence of the old but long since forgotten question about Paul's apostleship. Of late we have seen the attempt to discredit all of the Christian articles of faith by implying that they are merely Pauline flashes of ideas. Such characterization is simply absurd and demeaning. On the other hand, we cannot possibly view Paul's exclusion from the list of the apostles with indifference. In the first place, he has continuously been recognized throughout the church of Christ as an apostle; secondly, without his letters we would still have an apostolic gospel, but except for these we would lack an apostolic theology; and, finally, as we discover through more thorough research that we have neither more nor less assurance regarding the apostolicity of the writings of Matthew, John, and Peter than we have in the case of Paul's writings, it becomes clear to us that they inevitably stand or fall together. It quickly becomes clear that whatever verifiable assurance we have about the genuineness of the Gospels and letters we call apostolic depends upon historical testimonies concerning these men. Were they disciples of Jesus who by genuine signs proved their divine call? Have they really left us writings bearing their names? Here, in fact, the historical testimonies are all in agreement both with respect to Matthew's, John's, Peter's, and Paul's apostleship and the genuineness of the writings bearing their names. This is the witness of the ancient Christian church. It is either valid and therefore must be accepted, or invalid and therefore must be rejected in its entirety. Therefore, if we reject half of a historical testimony, we destroy the testimony in its entirety and reduce it to an untrustworthy story, constraining us to cull as truth only that which on other grounds is found to be reasonable. Since Luke, the oldest writer of church history, testifies with the same fervor to the genuineness of Paul's apostleship and to his apostolic ministry as he does in his witness to the apostleship of Matthew, Peter, and John, who were chosen by the Lord Jesus Christ himself, it is obvious that, if one cannot acknowledge Paul as an apostle on the basis of Luke's testimony, neither can one accept it concerning any other. However, in the case of Matthew, John, and Peter, we have no other historical assurance of the genuineness of their apostleship than the testimony of Luke, their own individual witness, and that of Paul. Moreover, not any single one of them has ever given himself a testimony as unequivocal as that which Paul gave on his own behalf. Consequently, they together with him and he with them must either be acknowledged as apostles or simply disavowed!

In other words, our Christian forefathers were neither in error by ascribing apostolic authority to Paul's teaching, nor by acknowledging the apostles' divine mandate to preach the true, unalterable Christianity. Wherefore, when they did not deduce any divergent teaching from Paul's letters their discernment was correct for there is none. Assuming that there had been one, it would have had to be given the same credence as if it had been explicitly stated in the Gospels. However, it is well-nigh inconceivable that several apostles, prompted by the same Spirit, would address themselves to the church in writing, and that one of them should expound a teaching for which there was no precedent in the writing of the others. Consequently, we do not discover any new tenets in Paul's writings. Notwithstanding, his writings do reveal a distinct and supplemental development both in his outline and interpretation of the basic truths of the Christian faith. However, this should not take us by surprise for in no way does Paul's testimony offer any additional guarantee of the trustworthiness of these fundamental truths. Therefore, the Spirit must have chosen him as a sacred writer for a different purpose, namely, the imparting and dissemination of knowledge and insight. It is perfectly in order, therefore, that even as the Gospels by their coherent testimonies instruct us concerning the essentials of Christian knowledge, so the New Testament letters, written by the apostles, inform us about those particular aspects of Christian truth which the Spirit deems proper for us, that is, the maturing Christian community, to know and acknowledge. This is my personal view. Others may, of course, think differently, but they are bound to admit that it is not Christian to find fault with the Spirit who impelled the apostles to write. Asking why we find only the framework of a Christian theology or why one article of the Christian faith is outlined and explained in far greater detail in one place than another, and simultaneously wanting to limit one's inquiry to the immediate occasion for the origin of most of the apostles' letters is tantamount to either denying that the apostles were called to teach the whole church, or equivalent to scoffing at the Spirit who guided the apostles in their writing and speaking. Indeed, he, who is the Spirit of God and of truth, knew well how to serve the first Christians in such a way as to benefit the entire church. The specific occasions for the writing of these letters and their literary form teach us that what is specifically addressed to particular groups of Christians cannot necessarily be enjoined upon all Christians. Therefore, the Christians' common confession of faith (the Apostles' Creed) should not be viewed as a mere compilation of verbal expressions and special affirmations drawn from various letters which at first neither were known to the whole church nor intelligible to any, except to Christians who already had attained a certain degree of Christian development and insight. Neither on this point did our Lutheran forefathers err, for their common confession of faith was in fact entirely evangelical, and their Augsburg Confession was exclusively for the theologians whom the forefathers rightly assumed to be sufficiently mature in matters of the Spirit to understand everything in the letters clearly calling for scholarly discernment. This limit upon the Augsburg Confession is so obvious that I do not even know for certain whether there is any doctrinal statement in the confession which is rooted solely in the developing Pauline theology. Even in regard to the Lord's Supper (Article X), where the need for Pauline definitiveness most often is apt to be felt by us, the Augsburg Confession does not move as much as a hair's breadth beyond what the words of the Lord declare in the Gospel according to Matthew (26:17–30). While the statements on orginal sin, free will, and justification by faith alone (Articles II, XVIII, IV) seem to be based entirely on Paul's unfolding theology, I have in the preceding pages shown that this is apparent rather than actual. That these confessional statements of necessity presupposed an evangelical theology ought to be grasped by anyone who is able to read them with an understanding mind, and as the church's theologians they should acknowledge the same in their discussion of these doctrines, even though they never were explicitly set forth by any of the apostles.

4

A Believing and Confessing Church

The first outcome of honestly taking upon oneself the task of reading the Scripture in order to determine whether the Augsburg Confession is genuinely Christian is that one reaches the immutable conviction that it is impossible to find any other teaching in the New Testament than that which our Lutheran forefathers openly acknowledged unless one deliberately imposes one's own view on the text. Once having made this discovery, one is easily tempted to believe that practically all theologians today are plain deceivers. All their followers are either like them or pure and simple animals in human form who do not feel even the slightest desire or need for any other bliss than that which the world offers. Consequently, they do not regard it as worth their trouble either to read the Scripture for themselves or take even a moment for a serious consideration of the question of eternal salvation. Such is the uncharitableness which we constantly are tempted to show as we presume to judge others, but if we are Christians we realize quickly that the temptation we should resist is, in fact, a display of self-conceit; wherefore, we also willingly excuse them because they are like sheep without a shepherd (cf. Mark 6:34). Doubtless, it is more difficult to excuse the theologians, for they cannot follow the example of the laity who, in their own spiritual sluggishness, simply forget what is written and what the message is. I do not know of a single example in which a layperson, having discovered the theologians' error and boldly protested the same, showed any inclination to really overcome the temptation to pass judgment upon the clergy. Apparently, the cause of such a situation is found in the sinful desire to excuse ourselves and lay the blame on others. This is one of the many reasons that as long as the possibility of the intrusion of flagrant errors faces the church, we need to foster the hope that erudite pastors will discover and courageously refute the errors. Therefore, if they are sincere about Christianity, they cannot help but realize that by cudgeling the erroneous and misleading theologians they are also striking the cudgel against themselves. Knowing that even selfishness sometimes prudently dictates reasonableness, wise people always act accordingly without, thereby, being one hair's breadth better than those whose selfishness impels them to do the opposite. Obviously, the honor for what such an opportune conflict may achieve belongs solely to the hand of him who governs all things wisely and guides the hearts like flowing streams of water wherever he wills. The temptation which faces us here is to commit another and far greater injustice, namely, to put the blame on human weakness and imperfection. Hereby, we actually impute all blame on him who always is righteous in his speech and perfect in his judgments. It is God, our creator and redeemer, on whom the burden of the consequences of our unconquerable weakness and inevitable blindness finally falls. Here, our selfishness does not draw us toward, but away from acknowledging the truth. Moreover, since the relationship between God and man is far less evident to all than the mutual relationship between human beings, we find it quite easy to blame God for everything without thereby giving the slightest semblance of blasphemy on our part. Yes, in our imagination we unintentionally fancy God as possessing characteristics typical of sinful and mortal creatures. Hence, on that basis, we either excuse him because he, as one of us, is unable to open our eyes to the truth, or we praise his love which causes him, again as one of us, not to lift a finger against his perverse children who find it

80

much more humorous to listen to one another's fables than to listen to the teachings of the Father. If we, in essence, have such an idolatrous heart that we have no intention of worshiping any other god but whichever one takes upon himself the responsibility of all of our evil and falsehood, or looks through his fingers and simply treats our wrongs as insignificant children's pranks, it becomes questionable whether we in this life ever will allow ourselves to be convinced of any guilt on our own part; thus merely obliging ourselves to excuse one another because we all are guilty, instead of either slyly or bluntly blaming God and declaring ourselves wholly innocent. However, if on the contrary and despite all our sinfulness, we really love the truth and desire to be servants of the true God, then we also trust him at his word and believe that before him neither the blindest among the heathens nor we have the slightest excuse. When we, on the basis of this faith, seek to explore the origin and growth of our errors, we perceive more clearly each day how foolish it is to blame God for what he demonstrably has shown that he completely hates and, therefore, has fought against and sought to prevent with all imaginable power when he in steadfast love determined to spare those who someday would be saved by grace. In other words, he refused to do what he bids all his servants not to do: root up the wheat along with the weeds (cf. Matt. 13:29). Wherefore, it is impossible for the highly learned among the Christians to acquire a thorough historical knowledge of Christianity and of the intermingling of errors and powerful attempts of winning over Christians to false beliefs, which are seen on all sides, without being completely convinced of the vindication of him who in the midst of the Christian communities "had a vineyard on a very fertile hill. He digged it and cleansed it of stones, and planted it with choice vines; he built a watchtower in the midst of it, and hewed out a wine vat in it; and he looked for it to yield grapes, but it yielded wild grapes" (Isa. 5:1–2). To our shame we must remain silent before him whose saving act, on our behalf, never can fail when we in all humility choose to be his fellow workers. On the contrary, it cannot possibly succeed if we, dominated by pride and egotism, despise our glorious calling and work against him, thereby destroying what he builds up! It is highly improbable that we ever can upset the plan of God; even if we were to make the attempt, it is not in accordance with his plan to grant obstinate sinners any part in the heritage of that son of Jesse whom we repudiate. In his own time, he leases the vineyard to better laborers who will consent to his plan and give him the glory! This is what he did with the vineyard in Palestine; and he obviously acted similarly each time that he, in the course of Christianity, moved the church and its seat of learning from the east to the west and from the south to the north. Indeed, we must be lacking in sound judgment, especially in spiritual matters and thus resembling dumb animals if we, even for a moment, were to imagine that when the Lord unleashes the storm the buildings by the North Sea are more secure than those by the Mediterranean Sea, or that he would look more calmly upon our bragging about our self-made Christianity for our own glory, in opposition to his word and in derision of his work and all of his guidance hitherto, than when he saw the very same occurring in Ephesus, Antioch, Alexandria, Corinth, and Rome! We tend, perhaps, to assume that he cannot see what is as clear as the noonday sun to his most humble servants, namely, that we are building a similar Tower of Babel, regardless of how skillfully we aim to construct it after the likeness of the Temple. Moreover, if we think that he, who discerns our "thoughts from afar" (Ps. 139:1), would permit himself to be deceived by the words which fall from our lips and by the empty reverence with which we speak of his only begotten Son, his (the Son's) unimpeachable Word, and his true church in times past, then to all appearances we toil, in the first place, to make Jesus Christ superfluous, second, the Bible fictitious, and third, the entire believing community of Christians with all of its thoughtful, clear-eyed, and heroic witnesses a vast throng of superstitious simpletons and outright fanatics who, contrary to sound reason, imagined themselves to be Christians. Is this what we have in view, or do we really mean that the Lord, who often by thunder and lightning has thwarted such delusions and trampled all such false teachings in the dust, now should have become too old, too weak, or too lenient to take such drastic action, instantly depriving so many upright and highly learned men of their good name and high repute? This, however, ought not surprise us when we know that Jesus Christ is the same today as yesterday, and that he will not under any circumstances be untruthful to his church and, thus, refute himself in order to spare the disbelieving theologians. Consequently, there is not the least justification for demanding that his followers and servants of the church should remain silent in the face of the awful distortion of the good of Jesus Christ which is perpetrated in widespread areas of Christendom for, as the Scriptures say, "at the name of Jesus every knee should bow" (Phil. 2:10). Having heard both his name and his word proclaimed "many who were paralyzed or lame were healed" (Acts 8:7). In the course of time, as the fame of Jesus Christ spread abroad, the believers were called Christians (cf. Acts 11:26), and they separated themselves from all those who either did not know anything about Jesus Christ, whom we worship, or they believed, according to their own reason, that they had a greater savior, master, and companion than he who was crucified could ever be. It is highly improbable that all of this can be widely publicized without causing great shame on all who took part in the distortion and boasted throughout the same of their love of truth, their unprejudiced reasoning, and their exemplary personal conduct and enlightenment. Not one of these claims can really be maintained; indeed, to seek to do this would be a despairing task. If one wishes to excuse oneself on the grounds of blindness and preconceived ideas, what then becomes of the enlightenment and freedom from prejudice? And if one desires to justify deception, motivated by self-interest, fear of others, and the wisdom of this world, what happens then to justice, to love of truth, and all the skillful cunning by which one hopes to transform the most un-Christian teaching into true Christianity? Should it surprise or offend anyone that we are the glory of the Lord Jesus Christ and his redeemed congregation, freed from the chains of darkness and the bands of error, who build our hope of eternal salvation on our sharing in Christ's sufferings (cf. Acts 9:15–16; Rom. 8:18) and in the power of his resurrection, both of which are far more precious than all the honor and affluence of the learned scholars who have labored to eradicate the Lord Jesus Christ's well-known faith both from the Bible as well as from the world? Is it not unreasonable to ask more of us who, spiritually speaking, are subjected to an overwhelming barrage of abusive language characterizing us as hating human beings, as being spokesmen for supernaturalism and apostles of darkness? For what are these epithets but the undeniable appellations of the servants of Beelzebub? How can it possibly be fair to ask more of us than that we, despite everything, remain quiet, patient, and sensible rather than retaliate by using similar abusive words? Instead, let us leave it to him who sees in secret and searches the hidden things of the heart to judge as to what extent unwittingly performed transgressions and contrived confusion have a part in this indefensible ploy with the most prominent, most holy, and clearly manifested life in the whole history of mankind. If there be any good reason to require more of us, it certainly cannot be that we should call that light which undeniably is darkness, or that enlightenment which clearly is obscure, or that openheartedness which unmistakenly is concealment, or that we as servants of the light and truth, bound by the vow of ordination, should disregard our pledge by failing to call everything spiritual by its proper name, regardless of how repulsive it may sound in the ears of the world! No, to do this would be to demand the impossible of us. Whether we are enemies or friends, we ought not to impose impossibilities, whether spiritual or physical, upon one another. In such cases, the very most which can be required of us is that we distinguish explicitly between God and ourselves; first, because neither God nor truth can ever be blamed for any errors; and, secondly, even though we have acknowledged the truth, we must never forget that we, too, "were straying like sheep" (1 Pet. 2:25). Moreover, we shall never be totally innocent of the hatred and derision which we, in the name of Jesus, must bear, for we shall never reach the state of perfection here below. We shall not be cleansed from the defilement of the human flesh and spirit until this tabernacle is dismantled. Then we shall become so imbued by the perfect love of God and his divine truth that self-love never again shall scintillate even in our most upright speeches whether they be to the glory of God, who is the very quintessence of purity, or a testimony concerning the Word which is as pure as silver refined sevenfold. It must be as clear to all as the noonday sun, whether friends or enemies, that we as servants of Jesus Christ and of his church must be either faithless traitors or inert cowards if we did not, in as bold and clearheaded manner as possible, insist upon Christianity's inalienable right to be and remain what it is and always has been. If in our discussion we obscure and confuse the significance of this point, it manifestly becomes as impossible for non-Christians to move from paganism to Christianity as for us to witness to its truth. Admittedly, it is meaningless to encourage people to become Christians and assure them that Christianity is true without first clearly having expounded what Christianity is and whereby it differs from all other religions in the world. Indeed, common sense causes us to blush on behalf of a generation which, while it calls itself enlightened, nonetheless holds such self-evident and fundamental truths questionable. In fact, many of this generation's scholars are not the least embarrassed by outright denying these truths. Such is the situation. Thus, we continuously encounter theologians who, indeed, assure us that their scholarly exposition of Chistianity sets forth the only true, right, and authentic Christianity. Yet, the moment we challenge them with the teaching of the Bible, they retract their words by insisting that it is totally impossible to decide what Christianity actually is. By this desperate method, the self-conceited, rationalistic theologians evade submitting any proof of the correctness of their interpretation of Christianity. Thus, in the eyes of the unlearned, the rationalists weaken all our clear proofs that, according to the Scripture, only our Lutheran forefathers' Christianity is truly genuine. Moreover, when the rationalistic theologians in their obvious adverseness to Lutheran theology declare the same to be superstitious, unfounded, contrary to reason, and demoralizing, they also seek to weaken our position: that their self-made Christianity, which is contrary to all Christian belief, is completely false and unauthentic; yes, it is but a distorted view of Christianity!

It is a sad state of affairs in which the church of Christ, especially since the beginning of the present century, finds itself. However, in the last century, the enemies of the church did not carry on their work in secret, as they do today, for in the eighteenth century it was commonly acknowledged by all that they were intent upon destroying Christianity. Today, on the contrary, the enemies of the church make bold to assume the appearance of advocates of genuine Christianity who merely attack that which is ungenuine, false, and demoralized in Christianity — Lutheran as well as Calvinist and Roman Catholic! It is a shocking experience for Christians to see this disheartening turnabout in the history of the church of Christ truthfully, briefly, and calmly described, in the year 1810, in the following passage:

> As one reflects, even briefly, upon the fact that no noteworthy apology in defense of the Christian faith has been published during the last ten years, one is certainly somewhat puzzled. However, this feeling recedes quickly as one considers that since the beginning of the earlier theological revolution, which has been continuous during the last two decades, a large number of theologians have moved so close to the thinking of the most scholarly opponents of Christianity that they have found very little to defend. The most distinguished among these theologians gave up the idea of being able to prove the accuracy of any prophecy as well as any Christian

doctrine which reason fails to comprehend; they either left the miracles to defend themselves or attributed only a slight significance to them, and they questioned seriously the existence of supernatural and direct revelation. However, regarding the church and the scripture they taught that every sound judge of Christianity must admit that the church's institutional function, under the guidance of providence, is to advance the moral life, and also admit that the Scriptures — along with the teachings of theological rationalism — contains sound moral principles.

Thus confessed the rationalistic theologian Heinrich Gottlieb Tzerchirner as recently as 1810. Strange to say, he was intent upon drawing the conclusion from church history that rationalism, in effect, was a going over to the enemies of Christianity whereby one surrendered everything distinctly Christian, and retained only the rationalistic conception of religion and those sound, moral principles which neither stand nor fall with Jesus Christ and the Christian revelation. Thus, only the shell of the Christian church was retained — a curious ruin which people somehow or other had become accustomed to visit, and where theologians quite conveniently delivered their moral deistic lectures. Surely, if we today were equally frank, much of the tiresome clash of words might have been avoided, and in no wise would people find me on the battlefield, for I believe him who says, "The power of death shall not prevail against it" (Matt. 16:18). I know only too well that if he himself no longer can defend the church, it follows that we are even far less equipped for the task. However, as I have written earlier, the time and the tempo have changed noticeably. Hence, I merely wish to call to mind how easy it was to foresee that this would follow the moment the Christian church, once again, had apologists whom the enemies of the church failed to beat to the ground, despite their scornful smiles and devilish nicknames. Whether or not we think of those theologians who had crossed over to the enemies of the church, or of those with whom they had entered into coalition, the apologists were bound to treat both of them alike and show them how impermissible it was to use an edifice for Christian worship as an anti-Christian lecture hall. Consequently, the rationalistic theologians who had joined the ranks of the enemy had only two choices: either to quit the church or in desperation insist that they are the church's legitimate proprietors, whereas the Christian apologists are malevolent heretics, religious fanatics, disturbers of the peace, and enemies of the church. Who will deny that the second position is but an implausible idea, so long as even one, single, believing Christian who possesses the necessary courage and eloquence is willing to show the ludicrousness and self-contradiction of such a position. Nonetheless, the rationalistic theologians have shown an increasing measure of self-satisfaction with their own position. Thus, it is not impossible but that a number of the younger followers of the school of rationalistic theology are so steeped today in this imaginary point of view as to conclude that either their self-made Christianity alone is genuine or it is completely impossible to state what constitutes authentic Christianity. For this reason, they claim the same right for the authenticity of their Christianity as we do of ours. This is an understandable assumption on their part, because they are many and we are few in numbers; they are erudite and we are stupid; they are highly learned and we have little or no learning. Consequently, every sensible person must forthwith think that what so many courageous, learned, and wise men promulgate as authentic Christianity necessarily must be so, unless the very question of what constitutes genuine Christianity is so murky and involved as to defy an answer. Indeed, if such be the case, it clearly is not even worth arguing about!

One must, indeed, be very inexperienced with the ways of the world if one does not know that this is the way by which most readers, both learned and unlearned, make short work of passing judgment on all who nowadays are determined to courageously defend the genuine Christianity against its spurious friends who have appointed themselves guardians of the Christian church, thus treating the church as if it were an old person who in his or her decrepit condition has lapsed into second childhood, and simply does not know what he or she is saying.

When we call these impetuous judges' attention to the binding obligation upon all Christian theologians to acknowledge the validity of the words of Jesus and his disciples which the rationalists clearly dispute, claiming that they successfully have rebutted the argument, then our rationalists immediately seek to teach those who are attracted to them how to answer us. They are to reply: Who says that we have even one, single, original word of Jesus which we can depend upon both as being genuine and as having been spoken in the context in which we find it in the New Testament? Moreover, as far as the apostles are concerned, it is very clear that they did not understand their Master. Hence their interpretations and applications are never unquestionable.

Our response hereto is that their argument has no bearing upon the question of what constitutes the true, that is, authentic Christianity. On the contrary, it is related to an entirely different question, namely, the question concerning the truth and trustworthiness of Christianity. Wherefore, whoever presents himself as a teacher of Christianity, and as such declares that Christianity is true, must either label himself as a deceiver of the people or insist that we have the words of Jesus in their proper context and that following Christ's resurrection the apostles became the authorized interpreters of his words. When we emphatically remind them of this self-evident truth, they face the inexorable alternative: either to make themselves an object of ridicule by insisting that the rationalistic understanding of what Jesus has said and thought is superior to that of those who heard him speak and were imbued by his spirit, or confess that the words of Jesus and his apostles indeed are valid. Even so, we are no closer because the rationalists still advocate that whenever people find themselves in this predicament they ought to be shrewd enough to answer: All right! The words of Jesus and his apostles are authoritative, but show us where the actual words are found. Prove that the so-called apostolic writings actually are of apostolic origin, and that they have been passed on unaltered. Also refute, if you can, the learned scholars' clear proof of the uncertainty of both the biblical canon and the New Testament writings. Their method of critical procedure is superbly illustrated by Johann Jakob Griesbach's (1745–1812) rules for determining the right reading.

Here, we surely have probable cause to reply: Whoever calls himself a Christian theologian must either become a deceiver or admit that we have a Christian revelation in the New Testament. This, obviously, would not be the case if the very genuineness of the New Testament writings, upon which our Christian knowledge depends, were uncertain. Consequently, whether it is right or wrong, wise or foolish, every theologian who desires to be regarded as a Christian must insist, despite all the learned scholars' objections, that the authenticity of all the writings which the ancient church has passed on to us is absolutely certain. Not withstanding the many variants, God who gave us the revelation surely also must have provided for its unaltered continuance in the church. Thus we can build on the words of this revelation in full confidence or create our own fantasies.

Thus, we rightly answer: those theologians who wish to retain their Christian identity cannot but admit the force of our point of view, if they really want to be logically consistent. However, in our enlightened and philosophical times, it has come to pass that theologians are not the least bashful about saying: We leave the strict consequents of the strictly logical and coherent reasoning process to the dull champions of orthodoxy, and freely confess that no enlightened theologian can be consequent. In all probability, we can most certainly prove that the knowledge which can be obtained by walking around in a fog and talking nonsense is scarcely worth the time and effort involved. Nor does such knowledge deserve any other praise than that which our satirists normally dedicated to the goddess of folly. Naturally, the highly learned among them link also this proof to a mistaken preoccupation with consequents on our part, making us appear as apostles of darkness whom the devil presumably has taught to bring the radiant enlightenment in ill repute. Of course, since the disciples are not above but subject to their masters, we are deafened by a loud, continuing outcry from all sides discrediting us, and asserting that it is far more reasonable to be inconsequent when there is no other way by which to avoid all the unreasonable assertions by which we make ourselves a laughingstock; and that it is perfectly all right to accept the New Testament as a divine revelation on which Christian theology must build exclusively and, at the same time, concede that we do not have a single actual word of God in the entire book, except it should be in the Letter of James, the genuineness of which has been disputed in the ancient church.

Even if we, armed with strong proof and bitter sarcasm, gradually were to succeed in convincing the rationalists that it is inappropriate to pretend to be priestly spokesmen for reason and at the same time make light of the importance of proceeding in logical consequence, there would still be questions which, even if answered, would be beyond the capacity of the common people to understand. In such situations it is always easy to confuse the crowd by resorting to evasiveness and highbrow, academic talk. However, even if this goal were achieved, the overall question would still remain because when there is no other recourse open they simply say, all right, we yield to all of your demands: the genuineness and trustworthiness of the books and the authenticity of the text. Here, we are speaking only of the original Greek text which reflects the extent to which the common speech of that time and region was influenced by Hellenistic, Greek-Hebrew usage; in nowise are we speaking about the German or Danish translations. We maintain that whoever has acquired a thorough mastery of the chief ancient languages and by this means has gained an adequate historical and philosophical knowledge of the thought and languages of the ancient Eastern world, that person—like we and our masters—is what you neither are nor ever will become, namely, truly erudite, temperate, and thinking philologists and philosophers. Indeed, such individuals recognize quickly that everything which you call the fundamental articles of Christianity vanish at closer examination as dew before the sunlight, or, to speak pointedly, as murky exegesis before the glowing torch of textual criticism; yes, as chaff before the wind, so the weariness of adherence to the letter vanishes before our life-giving spirit!

Even though we are not in the embarrassing position of not knowing what to answer, we know, however, that logical reasoning alone is not sufficient to convince the laity about the genuineness of Lutheran Christianity. All the well-founded objections which we, as Christian theologians, raise against the rationalists' insight as well as against the honesty of their procedure are intended to convince only our fellow theologians, never the laity of the church who would have to be as learned and wise as their teachers in order to assess their learning and insight. When we present the philosophical argument for the existence of a Christian revelation which all Christians necessarily must acknowledge, and if, according to circumstances well known to God, not one in a thousand is able to read it in the original language or study it according to the scientific principles of interpretation, it follows that God, therefore, must have seen to it that the lay people of the church never would be deceived by false translations; and, furthermore, God must have expressed his words concerning eternal salvation in such a way that the rendering thereof into all languages conveys the identical meaning to all thoughtful and serious readers. This proof is so complicated and deeply abstruse that few of the laity will have the requisite sharpness of mind to comprehend clearly the argument, especially as sophisticated objections to this process of reasoning cost little. Without doubt, the very most that we can accomplish by way of providing clear proof is to show that if the matter of dispute actually centers upon that which the rationalists insist on, then we ought never to speak about a

Christian theology but only about a biblical philosophy, nor would we ever be in a position to speak about a Christian faith but only about understanding and knowledge on the part of scholars, and, as for the members of the congregation, only about a blind belief in the understanding, knowledge, and integrity of either the whole body of ordained ministers or the nearest parish pastor. This much is clear to all, namely, that the rationalists, regardless of how skillfully they act, cannot escape the judgment that they are despairing papists who insist that we are saved by believing in one's own reason. Furthermore, they contend that the laity, under the threat of ecclesiastical ban, are not free to follow their own reasoning, but must make reason captive in obedience to the faith. Thus, the binding obligation which rests upon the laypeople is to believe—despite all human reason and understanding—that there is a divine revelation through which we finally, but only by enormous learning and diligent consideration of everything that will increase our knowledge, discover anew what we always have known. This wholly superfluous task of teaching people what they already know requires a very large number of bishops, ordained ministers, and professors in whose understanding the members of the congregation are to believe, despite their ever so much idle talk. Moreover, the lay people are called upon to believe in the existence of complete unity among the leaders, however much they contradict and refute one another. That all this self-contradictory hierarchism is the most crude and despairing papistry imaginable is easily proven. Hence, we absolutely disavow the ludicrous charge that we are aiming for a church hierarchy. The fact is that we, in contrast to the rationalists, take the genuine, Lutheran view that even the lowliest peasant may be as knowledgeable about the way of salvation as the most erudite bishop, for every honest translation is as helpful as the original text in enabling the reader to understand the way of salvation. Indeed, we fight hierarchism with those weapons which centuries of experience have proven effective. It is as clear as the noonday sun that, if there is a Christian revelation which only the pastors understand, then the pastors are the masters of the faith of the church, wherever the faith is found—in effect, masters of the whole church, spiritual and corporate. Who can blindly believe in the way of salvation which the pastors set forth but personally fail to follow, regardless of the cost? And if, occasionally, someone were to create a minor stir against a king who would refuse to dance to the piper, what then? If we were credulous enough to accept any opinion set forth by the erudite solely because of their learning, and they should affirm that the Lord's words, spoken in an Oriental language, mean the very opposite if spoken in our own language, then the scholars would need only to assure us that the same applies to the words: "He who resists the authorities resists what God has appointed . . ." (Rom. 13:2), and we would have to believe that it is Christian to rise up in rebellion!

We are quite certain that, as a result of this reasoning process, every thinking person must realize that the rationalists are clamorous philosophers whose special skill lies in receiving with one hand what they offer to give with the other, and in tearing down what they themselves erect. Moreover, if the rationalists' Christianity were truly genuine, then the genuine Christianity would be so repugnant that all people, except the clergy, would have to entreat God to keep them safe therefrom. Therefore, to employ this method for the purpose of convincing the unchurched rather than those who already are Christians—and so do not need to be convinced—of the absolute authenticity of our forefathers' Christianity is not likely to succeed. Without question, there are admittedly many, many people today who, while they do not profess the Christian faith, nevertheless show so much respect for Christianity that they would accept it, once it became clear to them what they would have to acknowledge if they did not wish to be regarded as the declared enemies of Christianity.

If, as a matter of fact, it is impossible for us to employ the strictly scientific method of the philologists and philosophers in order to convince the laity of the church that Luther's teaching is in accordance with the teachings of Christ, so it is similarly impossible for us to follow this method in order to convince the laity about the authenticity of Christianity. On the other side, it is an easy task for us to prove that what our opponents name Christianity is simply a sham and a self-contradiction. For the very present it may well appear as if we must either give up the hope of Christianizing anew our people or completely turn away from the scientific approach and option for the popular practical and moral approach, or whatever term we may apply to this particular way of inquiry whereby one proceeds not from the external, but from the inner experience—that is, not from Christianity as something which requires faith, but from the individual human being who stands in need of Christianity. Here the emphasis is less upon the mind's need for enlightenment than upon the heart's need for quietude and for an unimperishable hope of eternal comfort.

Undeniably, there is much that speaks in favor of exclusively following this way, because it seems to assure us that we can avoid all the stumbling blocks which the more recent enemies of Christianity have piled upon the ancient path of salvation— the path by which we most surely believe that we shall arrive at the goal. If Christianity is divine truth, it inevitably follows that it must have been fashioned exactly to meet the needs of the whole human race, rather than the particular needs of a few talented individuals or persons keenly interested in learning. The needs which all humankind have in common are: the need of a good conscience, and the need of comfort in all earthly suffering, including death and its sting which we who are alive and conscious of the human condition cannot but regard as the saddest of all deep-felt grief.

Indeed, some may object to this point of view by saying that if such be the case no one can become a Christian without being conscious of the need for that peace of God and eternal life which are granted to us through Christ Jesus. Granted that there are many who are wholly unaware of any such need, the answer to their objection is very simple; for the Lord himself gave us the answer when he said, "Those who are well have no need of a physician, but those who are sick" (Matt. 9:12); and "Come to me, all who labor and are heavyladen, and I will give you rest" (Matt. 11:28). Consequently, we should never seek to convince those of the truth of Christianity who manifestly have no feeling of any need for a Savior, for a divine word of grace, and for the gospel of peace. Any such effort on our part must either be ineffective or futile: ineffective because Christianity presupposes this awareness, and futile because Christianity is wholly unavailing in those instances in which the consciousness of one's need of that redemption which Christianity proclaims is lacking. The church of Christ ought never to lament the absence of those passers-by who have no felt need of the church's blessing because in their case it would be to no avail. Rather, the church ought to rejoice because it only finds those within its fold who recognize their need for the words of eternal life, and appreciate the fortunateness of having found in Jesus Christ what we never can succeed in finding anywhere else in the entire world!

At least this is the view of those of us who have believed and have come to the knowledge that Jesus is the Christ, the Son of the living God. Yes, we have experienced that it is utterly in vain to turn either inwardly on ourselves or to the eminently wise scholars for the ultimate answer to the soul's most holy envisioned desires and the heart's innermost longings: calmness in the midst of the storms of life, light on the mystery of the darkness of death, and spiritual power to overcome the temptations of the flesh. All of this we found in Jesus Christ, whom our forefathers worshiped as the Savior of the world. Yes, we have obtained all of these blessed fruits through a sincere faith in what our forefathers called "the Word of God," resulting in a living appropriation of and commitment to that Christianity which those who are contemptuous thereof scoff at and others, to wit, the majority of today's scholars, disdain and repudiate. As for the church in particular and for the human race in general, it may appear as if we who speak only because we believe (cf. 2 Cor. 4:13) could simply be indifferent not only to the gruesome game of words that some play with the sacred names of Christ and Christianity, but also toward the ridiculous extent to which they are willing to go in order to prove their point of view that no one knows what the book, the sayings of which they depend upon, actually sets forth. At first sight it may seem as if we were indifferent, but that is by no means the case.

It is irrevocably true that whoever is not convinced by what his own conscience tells him about his natural sinfulness, his inability to accomplish that which is good by his own strength, and his lack of any sincere desire for eternal life and happiness—such a person—will really never, in spirit and truth, become a Christian, for he is simply not conscious of any personal need for the forgiveness of sin, for a rebirth, or for a heaven-sent letter promising eternal life. The situation would remain the same, even if it were possible to clearly convince him that God literally had penned every word in the Bible, never allowing even the slightest change or deletion. On the other hand, to every believing Christian who from his own experience knows the divine accomplishments of the Christian faith, it must be absolutely certain that every human being who really is aware of his need and earnestly strives to resolve it will, indeed, come to believe in the gospel of peace and eternal bliss through which we and our forefathers have found rest for our souls! All this is true, indeed. Thus, if by an act of God this gospel actually makes amends for the needs of humankind, it is obvious that it must be a message of divine truth revealing what constitutes the true and authentic Christianity. We assume, of course, that this genuine Christianity corresponds to its own declared mission: to make this divine truth known which meets the spiritual wants of humankind. Thus, we bring our point of view to a reasonable and irrefutable conclusion. However, we ought not to conceal from ourselves that this approach leaves two questions wholly unanswered: namely, whether or not the teaching which we impart is genuinely Christian; and, second, whether or not Christianity in fact is the truth. For our sole purpose is to attempt to prove that the teaching which we impart, in the name of Christianity, is the divine truth about the way to salvation. Therefore, either it must be genuinely Christian or the authentic Christianity is simply not the divine truth leading us to salvation and, consequently, does not need concern us all. Here we clearly confuse two distinctly different questions: First, what is the divine truth which shows the way to salvation? And, second, what is true, that is, authentic Christianity? While the second question, in all other respects, may be unimportant as long as the first question is validly answered, it should not be a matter of indifference to us whether or not that which we, in our teaching, have made publicly known as Christianity actually sets forth authentic Christianity. Indeed, we all know that there is a religion, founded in the ancient past, which is called Christianity. We associate this Christian religion with everything that goes under the name of Christianity. In so doing, we undeniably confuse those to whom we address ourselves if what we proclaim, in the name of Christianity, in essence, does not exist. This, however, is by no means the only reason that it becomes imperative for us to do our part in adequately enlightening others about what constitutes the true or authentic Christianity. This is important because the individual's everyday experience and the wide range of experience which history narrates undeniably teach that people whose approach to their spiritual needs lies merely in the quest for the alleviation of their needs expose themselves to a thousand types of self-deceptions. Moreover, the same experience teaches that in the case of the teeming number of people, whose minds hitherto were unconscious of any felt need for reconciliation with God and for the hope of salvation, it was precisely due to the proclamation of a word, reliably attested to as conveying divine truth, that they were awakened to the realization of their religious need. The reality of the awakening experience to religious needs is seen already in the history of paganism. Despite the conscious religious needs on their part which caused them to believe in the conjured-up notions of paganism with the result that they were relieved, it was by no means the high, human need for peace of conscience and the hope of eternal life of which we speak. Yet, the history of Christianity's expansion into the non-Christian-ized parts of the world is the story of successive awakenings. Prior to this expansion, these people, who formerly had never felt any deep need for divine enlightenment and comfort, were satisfied with what, in fact, amounted to darkness and condemnation. But through the proclamation of the teachings of Christianity they were made very conscious of that deep void within themselves which Christianity promises to fill. From this we clearly conclude: first, that the individual human being is subject to the most tragic self-deception by reacting only on the basis of his or her natural needs; and, second, in order for Christianity to be effective, it is of utmost importance that it publicly discloses itself as the divine truth to those who up to this time have not had any personal experience of its glory. For this to be achieved, it is necessary to know what constitutes the true or authentic Christianity, because any prescribed doctrine must first be commonly known before any testimony to its veracity can be presented on its behalf. This becomes even clearer when we consider the history of Christianity because at the root of every religious quest within the Christian community, we discover the presence of a deep human craving for inward peace and for the hope of salvation. Moreover, we discover that whenever people, driven by this want, simply turned to the Bible in search of ways to rectify their condition without first having been enlightened about the true Christianity and the proper (i.e., Christian) use of the Bible, they invariably went sadly astray and created for themselves a pagan mythology in a Christian guise. Or to express it in the normal language of church history, they confused their own minds by subjecting themselves to unreasonably overpowering emotions and conjured-up notions of the mind. Indeed, the cause of this aberration is easy to discover, for as one starts from the spiritual needs of which one is conscious, it is obvious that one is proceeding not only from the innermost but also the darkest recesses of human existence. This impenetrable depth—the depth of the heart—must, therefore, be perfectly clean and unaffected with disease if we, by relying exclusively upon the longings and impulses which arise therefrom, were to succeed in seeking and apprehending the truth. At this point, however, it is quite obvious that whenever we at heart feel the need for reconciliation with God, for strength through divine power (cf. Eph. 6:10), and for the hope of eternal life, then it becomes clear that the heart, in effect, is far from clean and unaffected by infectious disease, because everything which is clean is pleasing to God, requiring neither divine reconciliation nor purification. Wherever the natural needs exceed the innate treasure, there exists a disproportionate relationship, which cannot possibly have been originally intended, but must have been caused by an act of sin resulting in a break of the natural order of things which is the work of the all-good, all-wise, and all-powerful creator. Hence, even as the person who is absolutely guiltless can feel neither the pangs of conscience, nor experience any remorse characterized by an awareness of the need of grace and forgiveness of sin, so likewise it is impossible for any created human being to experience the need for something higher than that which human beings by nature are able to want and achieve. Thus, man's corruption is seen not only in his powerlessness to help and comfort himself, but also in the voice of conscience charging us with enmity between ourselves and our creator. Now if a man be corrupt, he is indeed a sinner, and it follows that the power of sin is precisely most dominant in the murky depths of the human heart where even by the light of nature it is not recognizable. Who can doubt but that even the best impulses which arise from the human heart are mixed with uncleanness? Yes, they are contaminated and cannot, therefore, be followed blindly without our going astray! Hence, is it not surprising that all those who definitely feel the need of grace, restoration, and renewal of the hope of eternal life, according to the image of him who created us, should turn to the Christian revelation for counsel, and yet fail to inquire about what constitutes the true, that is, authentic Christianity? Rather than pursuing this question, they merely want to follow the inclination of their hearts and base their opinion of what is genuinely divine upon their subjective experience. No wonder they were misled and formed in their own minds such notions concerning the Christian faith, regeneration, renewal, and the general order of salvation which not only appealed most to them personally, but also appeared capable of being reconciled with the sinful tendencies dominating their lives. Small wonder, indeed, when a sinful human being blindly following his murky feelings dreams, even in the midst of sinning, that he is pure and blessed!

These are the ever-inescapable consequences of viewing Christianity as something indeterminable, except as this question is settled through the individual's own inner experience. As we contemplate these things more deeply, as they indeed deserve, we discover that those who think that feeling, per se, can determine what constitutes divine revelation may, on the same basis, very well deny man's need of revelation, even as those who insist that their reason and comprehension constitute the measuring stick and final test of divine truth. Thus, the difference between the two groups is that the former unpremeditatedly follows the false imagination which they state formally in the readily comprehended concept: the individual human being's own inner light is all-sufficient. However, if that actually were the case, there would be no limit to the extent to which the debate might continue as to whether this inner light is attributable to the power of imagination, feeling, or reason. In short, whether it is to be found in the head or heart, it is certain that in either case man does not stand in need of any supernatural revelation. For that reason, it is in order that our self-opinionated people deny this need, and that they, in addition, also deny the need of reconciliation with God, of the forgiveness of sin, and of salvation by pure grace—all, of course, an entirely natural consequence of their position. If mankind had been endowed by nature with both a reliable inner guide to truth and an impelling force which the individual person, without prior scrutiny, only needed to follow in order to achieve his or her temporal and eternal goal, then mankind would not have fallen into sin and corruption, as none was a sinner. If, nonetheless, mankind was found to be sinful, the fault was not mankind's but God's. However blasphemous and self-contradictory such a contention may be, yet it lies more or less hidden in every teaching which, while admitting to error and mismatched relations on the part of human beings, still insists that these conditions can, if necessary, be discovered and corrected in a natural way, and that, therefore, a supernatural light and supernatural regeneration and renewal are just as superfluous as the actual forgiveness of sin.

Under these circumstances it really seems as if not only the Christian church but also the entire question of man's salvation are in a despairing situation. Even if we were willing to forgo the question concerning authentic Christianity and limit our discussion to that of the true enlightenment and what it teaches about eternal salvation, we would still be just as embarrassed, because textual criticism has made the Bible unserviceable as that light in darkness which it was, indeed, to our Lutheran forefathers, lay and learned alike. It is obvious that when a book is intended to enlighten us about something whereof we have no previous knowledge, it must be taken literally. This, of course, is not to say that one, without sense and reason, tears the words out of their context, or gives them a significance which they only could have if the book either did not center upon the elucidation of questions of divine nature, or dealt with entirely different items. This is simply an awkward method of interpretation by which one, literally speaking, takes the words as they chance to fall without inquiring whether, according to one's judgment, the meaning which the words convey is reasonable or unreasonable, but only ask whether it is clearly understood. Therefore, as soon as one questions the genuineness of the original words, the accuracy of their translation, or the meaning of the message itself, the book undeniably ceases to be a light and becomes obscure, requiring a light from some other source for its clarification. Thus, if it cannot be denied that the Bible is an obscure book, especially in the eyes of all who nowadays must be convinced about the truth that leads to eternal blessedness, it becomes obvious that there is no way in which we, unaided, can try our hand at enlightening anyone either about the truth concerning eternal blessedness, or about authentic Christianity. Even if we, on the basis of the Bible's own testimony, could prove its divine origin, it would be of no avail unless we also could point to the Bible itself for evidence as to what this revelation of divine origin contains. Thus, if once and for all the light of the church actually were extinguished, then every one of us who feels the need for something over and above that which the world can give and our reason comprehend, must either become a scholar in order to discern a guiding light in the Scriptures, or blindly follow what he finds most prudent: one's own feeling or another person's testimony concerning the way which led him or her to find light and life. However, to think of a church body proper under such circumstances is simply futile, unless some person's individual confession of faith were to be elevated to the level of an article of faith, necessitating the church members' rigid adherence. Moreover, any conversation or discussion would have to be limited to questions of private concern like those, for example, between an apprentice and his foreman or that of an audience and its invited lecturer. It stands to reason that whatever a secular power might achieve by way of coercing a confession of faith where faith actually is wanting, or demanding an outward appearance of agreement where none actually exists, cannot be taken into consideration in any discussion where the issue is not about appearances, but actuality—not about words which fall freely from the lips, but about man's deepest needs, namely, his spiritual and eternal welfare.

If we are familiar with church history, we know that this discouraging situation, which is not new, goes back to a remote period. The Reformation clearly sought to allow lay people to read the Bible by themselves and thus become enlightened by "the heavenly light." Second, the Reformation sought to guard against making the teachings dependent upon the individual's own feelings, sharpness of mind, and affirmed standpoint. While the Reformation did not succeed in healing the deadly wound, it did cover the wound with a bandage, thereby making it more bearable, but also, at the same time, delaying the breakup which we have experienced. By any impartial consideration, it must be admitted that it was not by way of destroying the papacy, but only by eliminating the most serious abuses of papal authority and by making it more dependent upon collegiality and placing it under a fixed, procedural rule, that the papacy became more tolerable for the present time. For any church body which is dependent upon something other than the members' conviction has only an alluring appearance of unity, because the faith, upon which all depends, does not permit itself to be pressed upon any person any more than it itself will ever resort to force. The confession of faith without belief is, even on the part of the most honest persons, only empty and indefensible talk. As was the case concerning agreement in matters of faith, it should be noted that the situation was the same, especially among the lay people, with respect to their understanding of either the nature of authentic Christianity or the truth which leads to salvation. Here, we face two questions which all the Reformers and their disciples failed to separate; they constantly failed to differentiate between the two or combined them into one. For after all, what assurance did the lay people have of the genuineness of the Bible, or the correctness of the translation, or the meaning of the words, except the explanation by the pastors? Moreover, what layperson was in position to analyze and understand the entire content of the Bible so as to be able to judge for himself whether the so-called erudite tenets of the scholars in every respect were in full accord with the Bible? In all probability the pastors came much closer toward achieving this goal because of their education in the original languages of the Bible, history, and the scientific method as it applies to same, hopefully enabling them to convince themselves of the origin, the content, and the accuracy of the translation of the Bible. However, even here, knowledge and agreement were far more assumptive than real, partly because only a relatively small number of the pastors had advanced far enough in their study of the original languages of the Bible to possess the skillfulness and insight which undeniably are required in order to properly understand what one reads. Moreover, the seeming agreement was to a large extent artificially effected by the symbolic books and an accordingly flexible system of dogmatics. In effect, the symbolical books were, at the very best, the common source for drawing temporary knowledge about true Christianity and the way of salvation. Consequently, the reader had to make a choice: either to contend that the authors of these books were directly enlightened by divine inspiration, in which case the symbolical books, and not the Bible, actually became a revelation, or admit that one's knowledge of Christianity and salvation was based upon a mere human witness, namely, the writers' witness as to what constituted the Word of God and as to how to convey its meaning. Who does not see here the beginning of the now ruling exegetical anarchy and hierarchy of eminent scholars under which every scholar assumes for himself the unrestricted freedom to determine both what the laity shall believe and shall reject? Who does not realize that this would be the inevitable development either as soon as the secular government permitted the theologians to freely express their own views, or as soon as these scholars had the courage and power to break the ban upon freedom of speech, the legality of which they did not acknowledge? On the other hand, there are the lay people who, ever since the Reformation, have been encouraged to believe in their ability to see and read, but now lately have become convinced that they in reality have been seeing things through the eyes of the pastors rather than their own. This has resulted in their refusal to continue to follow blindly the pastors' pronouncements any longer. At a time when the pastors openly and loudly contradict one another, it is simply impossible for the lay people to do otherwise. Thus, it really looks as if the thought of a church body in an inner, spiritual meaning must be given up. Moreover, any attempt to save the shadow thereof by making prescribed ceremonial services obligatory can never be the wish of others than those who either regard their own respective office or the external disciplinary rules as of greater worth than the freedom of conscience.

As far as the church and revelation are concerned, the situation appears to be so despairing that the enemies of both have used it as the very basis of their sure hope that the church and revelation will come to an end. It is on this foregone conclusion that those theologians take their stand, who in an un-Christian way charge all who in a practical way seek to lead others to the faith of the forefathers with being mystical and fanatic enthusiasts, whom the secular authorities ought to silence in order to ensure peace and unity in the church. Under the present circumstances, this clearly means that the prevailing dogmatic and exegetical views among the theologians can continue unchallenged and, as far as possible, even be forced upon the church, that is, the congregation. Certainly, no believing biblical scholar can remain silent in the face of today's dominant dogmatic and exegetical views. But even if the un-Christian characteristics of these views cannot be definitely proven, they are nevertheless wholly unacceptable, because they are contrary to undeniable truths, besides being self-destructive. However, even so, very little would be gained thereby, unless it also were possible to convince all truth-loving people that what the forefathers called Christianity was in truth what the name designates. Indeed, it is highly improbable that any believing biblical scholar today would be as fortunate as Luther and his helpers were in getting their testimony concerning authentic Christianity elevated to a rule of faith. Even if their achievement might be repeated, it is most unlikely that any one, among the believing biblical scholars, would take the risk involved in repeating the venture which, however commendable, may be viewed from many different standpoints, resulting in turn in divisions within the organized church body instead of achieving the incontestable goal: namely, once again to unite anew everything genuinely Christian in the church as it was in the beginning.

Ever since the Reformation it has become commonplace to say, "In matters of faith, have no regard for any human testimony, but do give due regard to the divine witness." In the intervening time, however, we have come to realize that this was merely a cliché, since the theologians, in striking contrast to the saying, clearly did build upon an obviously human testimony: that of the Reformers. Strictly speaking, their testimony was entirely invalid because they sought to have it regarded as the only correct way of interpreting the Bible, something which lies beyond any human being's testimony, without oneself being inspired. Once we recognize this and also reflect upon the fact that the propagation of Christian knowledge is carried on by human witnesses and, finally, that any talk about a divine witness or testimony without miracles is simply idle speech, then we are on the right way to discover what clearly must be found: another method than that commonly used to convince those who do not know, but earnestly seek to learn what constitutes authentic Christianity. These are the only people that our discussion centers around, and we are deeply concerned about them — even to the point of not regarding those who only ask, "What is Christianity?" in the same cynical vein as Pilate asked, "What is the truth?" (John 18:38).

As soon as we realize that we need a trustworthy human testimony in order to obtain certainty as to which form of Christianity is true, that is, genuine, then we know too where to find such a testimony, because if the church actually has a history, the testimony must perforce be found in church history. It would have been impossible for Christianity to have had a history with no one being knowledgeable of its teachings. If such, indeed, actually had been the case it would have been impossible to either confess or deny Christianity and, indeed, still less likely that it would have accomplished anything worthy of remembrance.

It is really strange that it ever should have been necessary for us to make this discovery. However, once having made the discovery, it becomes clear that it is in church history alone that we find the dependable source of knowledge concerning the essence of original Christianity which, of course, must continue to the end of the world to be the only true or authentic Christianity. Far from turning us away from the Bible, this discovery, on the contrary, enables us to take the right approach to the reading of the Bible and to find within its pages a trustworthy testimony concerning the knowledge we are seeking to acquire. We accept the historical books of the New Testament for what they first and foremost are, namely, a human testimony about the founding of the Christian church and the origin of the name Christian. In other words, what we have here is the oldest church history which—provided that it is not a grossly fraudulent misrepresentation—is contemporaneous with the recorded events. The coauthors of this history are, first, the earthly builders of the church, that is, the apostles, and next their disciples. We view the four Gospels and the Acts of the Apostles for neither less nor more than they claim to be, a truthful and dependable history of the life and teachings of Jesus Christ and his chief apostles, and of the initial beginning of the expansion of their teaching. In so doing we undeniably escape all the difficulties the theologians among our forefathers became involved in as they, without the slightest justification, insisted that what we have before us here is not a human but a divine testimony; neither is it a history, but a revelation. This completely unfounded and misoriented position, whereby the church-historical point of view was thrown into disorder, had the tragic consequence that the theologians by their preconceived opinion and indefensible interpretation sought to conceal that inconsistency in trivial matters which actually increases the historical reliability of the Gospels. In their opinion, a divinely revealed word could not possibly allow for any inerrancy. Assuming now that the historical books of the New Testament are authentic, then we have an unquestionably valid source of knowledge to enlighten us about the original and only true Christianity. Even if the apostles' account of the Lord's ministry and Luke's story of the work of the apostles' labor in propagating Christianity were shown to be unreliable, these writings nevertheless would still constitute a reliable source of information concerning the true or authentic Christianity, for it is irrefutable that the apostles and their first disciples were the first Christians, regardless of whether their Christianity was true or false, or brought into existence by way of honesty or crookedness. Thus, as their Christianity uncontestably is the original, it is also the only true Christianity. Thus, whoever publicly dissents therefrom, yet assumes the name, is simply an impostor.

Once we recognize that the four Gospels and the Acts of the Apostles indeed are the work of the first Christians, it becomes clear that in all fundamentals the oldest and only true Christianity was the very same that we affirm in the Augsburg Confession—both struggling against the same adverse views. This is the position which I adamantly have maintained and sought to demonstrate. However, I might have been far more clear-cut if I had given the survey of evangelical Christianity from a purely historical point of view; instead, I merely presented it as a cautious Lutheran theologian who did not dare to separate the question concerning the nature of apostolic Christianity from the question of the apostles' own words in their writings.

By distinguishing between these two questions we make it possible for all Greek New Testament scholars, who really desire to learn what constitutes authentic Christianity, to reach a common point of view because the Gospels' narrative style is so plain that the textual meaning cannot be doubted. Moreover, the ancient church's testimony concerning the genuineness of the Gospels is so well-founded that no one who knows the testimony can ever doubt its validity, unless he or she finally decides to doubt — a step which no thoughtful person would ever take. We know full well that there are times when we, without any apparent self-contradiction, find ourselves casting doubt upon everything historical, even our own state of existence.

If this is the situation as far as scholars are concerned, what about the lay people? Is it possible to assert that this testimony actually is intended for the laity and has been passed on to them by way of others than the scholars who assure them saying, We have found it thus? No, in the opinion of the lay people, it is only a testimony by scholars in whom they place far less faith than their forefathers showed the theologians of their day. Honest lay people can serve as valid witnesses about these things, but when their testimonies are boldly contradicted by other scholars they may, against their own will, succumb to doubt.

By taking the historical approach, we have wrested the key of knowledge from the professional theologians who wrongfully have used the key to lock the door of the church which they have been called to open. Moreover, we have deprived those of the key who themselves not only refuse to enter, but even prevent others from entering. Yes, we have offered the church's key to all educated persons who are able to read Greek, and who consider it worthwhile to inquire into church history about the light of the church! A great deal is unquestionably gained hereby, especially at a time when the university student enrollment is high, the curriculum in Greek is greatly improved compared with years ago, and church history is now an optional subject and open to all. When the church must formulate its Christian knowledge on the testimony of certain scholars, it becomes obvious that such a testimony is far less apt to be regarded with suspicion if the scholars' motive for testifying has no other purpose than that of enlightening their fellow lay members about the truth. It is clear as sunlight that a scholarly lay person whose relation to the church, by his own choice, is no different from that which every Christian has to his fellow Christians, is a far more independent and unbribable witness about what he has learned from church history than some of us who have served as teachers in the church, imbued with the discipline of a certain school of theology with its particular obligations and points of view. Some may contend that this gain is more seeming than actual, because, nowadays, the educational elite among the lay people seldom worry much about Christianity. It is possible to meet this objection in several ways. The objection simply cannot be sustained when one considers how easy it actually is for the educated lay person to follow his inclination to learn Greek in order to personally become a trustworthy witness, testifying to that which he has felt to be lacking.

If there were no other way whereby the entire church could obtain a valid testimony concerning the true and authentic Christianity, then it should be a matter of highest priority, on the part of all Christian scholars, to extend the knowledge of Greek among church people wherever possible, or at least make the youth acquainted with the history of the early Christian church, the Greek alphabet, and the use of a dictionary so that in case of uncertainty they may make an informed judgment. However, even if such a goal cannot be attained, we shall have the satisfaction, at least, of knowing that we have done our very best to build the church's professed convictions upon a firm foundation. In general, those who have neither desire nor aptitude for such schooling are inappropriately prepared for the task of distinguishing between reliable and unreliable testimonies; instead, they are guided by feeling.

By taking this approach, it is certain that the church will make progress in its task of furthering Christian enlightenment. While this advance in Christian enlightenment so far has not completely succeeded in doing away with the centuries-old, oppressively serflike conditions of the church under the Roman papacy, nevertheless it has eased the burden which the people have lamented. Among us, at least, the people's reaction to the theological controversies and the predominantly strict orthodoxy of the Lutheran Church in Saxony has been one of understandable patience. However, their response to the rationalists and their teachings has been a loud, heavenward cry. This is certainly well-known. Moreover, it is also clear that the question concerning the church's Christian enlightenment must be a matter of conscience on the part of scholars. Here, we shall not hide the fact that it will take a long time before the fruits of this effort will be seen. Hence, the church needs immediate help in order to overthrow the rationalists' papal-like yoke without simultaneously falling prey to some fanatical anarchy's terrible aberrations.

Hence it is very evident that in the case of serious-minded persons of all parties and confessions, the intellectualization of Christianity is definitely not beneficial to any one who in his or her own heart refuses to take lightly both the qualms of conscience and the anxiety about eternal salvation. Day by day it becomes increasingly clearer that the hearts of a great many people tremble because they have a sense of guilt. Regardless of what the theologians may declare, the hearts of such people are on the brink of despair, if indeed there be no Gilead balm for the healing of human hearts by a word of grace from above and through a living hope of salvation. What will the consequences thereof be at a time when people's confidence in the Word of God as recorded in the Scriptures is shaken to the very foundation, let alone when in a sense faith in only one credible method of interpretation has almost totally disappeared and apparently become irrevocably lost? What about the consequences thereof? According to the laws or order of the human mind and spirit on one hand, and according to the centuries-old testimonies of history and experience on the other hand, the effect can only be that all who, in varying degrees, worry about salvation or, at least, seek a pause in the spiritual battle of the hearts, will either leave the way open for themselves to interpret and apply the Scripture according to the desire of their own hearts, or they will select a great number of teachers who tickle the ears of their listeners and thus excite their minds beyond control, causing them to become the targets of religious fanatics who, under the guise of Christianity, zealously seek adherents to their exciting and bizarre way of salvation. The rationalists' ice-cold and distorted moralizing is communicated to all in what undeniably resembles a dead language, not the least to the simple-hearted to whom it is completely unintelligible. Hence the question arises: Do the rationalists, even if there were an alliance between them and the parties in power, really believe that they are able to prevent the spiritually distressed from seeking comfort wherever they believe that they may find it, or from expressing their joy once they think that they have discovered it? If the rationalists take this stand, then they have been overpowered indeed by the blindest superstition that the world has ever seen. For in such a case, they believe—despite all sound reason and history's clear and valid testimony—that in the world of the spirit one can extinguish the burning oil with water; yes, that the flesh can kill the spirit; and that the oil which one casts upon the fire will not cause it to spread, but keep it under control.

We who believe and know in whom we trust can neither be blind to the threatening storm nor so foolish as to think that it can be turned away at the tinkling sound of brass and bells. The very thought that we ourselves in a practical way may appear to give, if not our approval, then what may be somewhat similar, namely, encouragement to those who follow the desire of their own hearts is, indeed, cause for concern on our part. We cannot possibly see ourselves as standing between those of systematic unbelief, on the one hand, and those of a rather undisciplined life of godliness, on the other hand, without anxiety on our part. For even when we labored most ardently and our efforts were crowned by the most desirable results, we still were beset by the fear that we might not have led that group that gathered together about the word of life, which we proclaimed, into the unmovable and indivisible church of the Lord Jesus Christ, but only into a particular school of thought which, even though it may be built upon the church's foundation, nevertheless is but a human accomplishment that like a cloth of fabric inevitably is bound to age and disintegrate into dust. How well I know that our self-appointed teachers of religion label all such worries if not as being completely hypocritical, then at least over-zealous. Yet, what else should we expect to hear from those who have no living perception of the human condition under which we are only something in the sight of the all-seeing God when we in our own eyes are nothing, while the Lord, who is our light, our salvation, and our strength of life, is all-important to us, including his honor, his victory, and his crown! Of this I have had a living awareness. Thus, in the midst of my anxiety for the scattered flock, it became clear to me that I must not allow myself to be revered as the shepherd of the flock, even if it appeared as if I had achieved such a standing. Second, I recognized that I had no right whatsoever to lead anyone to any other than to him whose hired servants we all are—servants who run away in fear of the wolf and are incapable of defending ourselves, let alone the flock. It was during this period that I discovered the most rewarding testimony for all of us, both lay and learned. Specifically, I am speaking of that living testimony in the church of Christ which was passed on by word of mouth from one person to another. Despite many changes in the course of time, it remained both unaltered and independent of all schools of thought and ecclesiastical party lines within Christianity.

Now my sorrow had come to an end; my sadness was transferred to joy, because now I could answer every person who asked me about the essence of the true, that is, authentic, Christianity without first demanding trust in my personal honesty, not to mention my faith, knowledge, and insight. Now I can ask each questioner: Am I not right in assuming that when you inquire about the true Christianity, then you are thinking about the Christians' faith and hope? For, otherwise, Christianity really does not mean anything to you and your question really becomes a matter of indifference to me. However, if your leading question be that of the faith and hope of the Christians, the answer is clear-cut. The fact is that unless the Christians down through the centuries confessed the faith and hope that the very first Christians publicly professed and affirmatively responded to in Holy Baptism, then they simply had nothing, neither faith nor hope. But to draw such a conclusion in light of the uncountable millions who confessed this very faith and hope is most uncharitable and blatantly ignorant, especially considering that many of them regarded their confession of faith as more precious than life itself. Yes, indeed, if only one of them had the faith and hope which they all confessed, then that individual undeniably possessed the one and only true Christianity. It is undeniable that whoever really believes and hopes what all Christians confess is, indeed, a true Christian. On the other hand, those who might confess over and over again, but neither believe nor hope what they say, are either hypocritical or simply talk nonsense.

As for the church's testimony of faith, the most erudite among the scholars may snicker as much as they please. The fact still remains that it obviously is not possible to point to a more authoritative testimony concerning what the early Christians believed and hoped with respect to the true, that is, authentic, Christianity. Even the most extensive examination of all the books in the world will not lead to any discovery worthy of comparison, for we have no desire to convince those about the nature and implications of the Christian faith who take pleasure in doubting, but only those who are troubled by doubt and earnestly wish to know what one must believe in order to be a Christian.

Of course we are speaking about the Apostles' Creed, which the theologians, with some semblance of being correct, object to on the grounds that the Creed in effect is so limited and so indefinite in form that its testimony with all its incontestable authority, nevertheless, is insufficient. However, the answer is quite simple because for the person in danger of drowning every single sensation of touching something stirs hope of rescue whether it be but the smallest deep-rooted twig on the bank of a river or a boat, however small and unsturdy. Today, the question of what constitutes true Christianity has become very complicated, not only on account of many unavoidable quarrels, but because many theologians' very scholarly and diligent work on this subject has become so intricate that even the well-educated who, at least to some degree, are able to unravel the complex questions must be thankful, indeed, for their advantageous position. Yes, at a time when people in all seriousness ask about Christianity, there is ample reason on the part of all inquirers to count themselves inexpressibly fortunate in having discovered that the answer to the question has been given by truly trustworthy lips: in this matter the voiced declaration of the entire Christian church. Even though this answer may leave some questions unanswered, the fundamental Christian knowledge, which the church found all sufficient, cannot be regarded as inadequate unless the Christian faith itself is wholly insufficient as a way of salvation. After all, this is the faith which the church confesses, and whoever is anxious, in ever so small a degree, about his or her salvation surely will be reluctant to pronounce that knowledge inadequate which points to the way of salvation, even though there may be many other things that he or she gladly would like to know more about.

My only purpose in saying this is to show how easy it is to refute the scholars' numerous and sophisticated objections to the simple wording of the church's faith. I find that what they label as the inadequacy of the Apostles' Creed is precisely one of its great and praiseworthy features; it does not separate Christians, but unites them as shown by the remarkable way in which the Christian theologians, even in the midst of the most raging controversies, yet were in mutual agreement about its essential function. Admittedly, this confession of faith also can be misinterpreted. On the other hand, whoever is able to coin words which elude misinterpretation, obviously, must be wiser than God. Since none of us can make such a claim, it behooves us, indeed, not to dabble in any human attempt to outshine the work of God. Instead, we should simply rest assured that when the Church of Christ—despite all misinterpretations and distortions of its Creed and Scriptures—still stands immovable, then our hope for its future is well grounded. With this hope in mind, we gladly comment: what the Apostles' Creed, with its historical form and matchless clarity of thought, seeks to express cannot be misunderstood except by deliberate falsification far greater than any human being's power to pull this weed out by the roots. It is quite true that there are faithful Lutheran pastors who feel, even as I have felt, that the Creed omits any mention of several aspects of Christian thought and decisions which, in their opinion, are all but indispensable. Nevertheless, one would have to be a non-Christian if, on the basis of one's own view, one were determined on defying the apostolic church which, with the necessary consent of the apostles, pronounced the Creed sufficient for their need. In effect, they declared that, upon one's own responsibility, every Christian must have the right to make his own judgment with respect to every question that the Creed does not settle; he is free to interpret the Scriptures, according to his own ability to judge wisely, without either being deprived of the name Christian, or excluded from the community of believers. In all probability, Roman Catholic priests surely will be more conscious than we of the loss of many more, in their eyes, indispensable decisions if the Apostles'

Creed were to become the supreme rule of faith in the church, thus eliminating papal primacy and infallibility and allowing Christian freedom in the task of biblical interpretation, as well as in the matter of the church's way of worship. Of course, it could happen that the theologians of that party which constantly championed the apostolic church and most fiercely rebuked us for showing lack of respect for it — a charge which we cannot entirely deny — might turn out to be far slower than we to show true regard for the apostolic church by discontinuing the practice of viewing all later doctrinal formulas, authorized in the course of time, as articles of faith which, in addition to the Apostles' Creed, must be accepted and confessed by everyone. However, in agreement with Martin Luther, we freely say that we have not added anything except what, according to our absolute conviction, is in unison with the very first statement of faith and clearly founded upon the Word of God, which the apostolic church put into our hands to be for each of us: "A lamp to my feet and a light to my path" (Ps. 119:105). What difference does it really make whether the biblical scholars, here and above, are either willing or slow to let the truth rule, as long as those who are inquiring about Christian truth know where to find it? Whom does the willingness and slowness really benefit and hurt? It benefits and hurts, as the case may be, those who choose to foster and practice either willingness or slowness. Is the Lord absolutely dependent upon any one of us? Considering that the Spirit has begun the good work in the church and has continued it effectively without any interruption throughout the centuries, is it reasonable to conclude that he, if we were to fail, would lack the wisdom, power, and means whereby to bring his work to its completion at the day of the Lord Jesus Christ? All Christians know what to answer, and all pagans will be obliged to recognize that we, who bend our knees in the name of Jesus, and honor the Son, even as we honor the Father, are not worshiping a pagan god. We do not depend upon what is in the wind and weather, nor upon our own virtue and wisdom, but we do believe in the Holy Spirit, Christ's true advocate in the world, who is powerfully able to preserve the church and to bestow upon all those whom he therein unites the forgiveness of sins, the resurrection of the body, and the life everlasting. Amen.